**UNCLASSIFIED**

USAF DEPLOYMENT PLANNING FOR SOUTH

1966

(U)

by

Jacob Van Staaveren

USAF Historical Division Liaison Office

June 1967

**UNCLASSIFIED**

# UNCLASSIFIED

### FOREWORD

USAF Deployment Planning for Southeast Asia, 1966 is the fifth in a series of special historical monographs on the war in Southeast Asia prepared by the USAF Historical Division Liaison Office.

After discussing briefly Air Force views on the strategy for the war, the study describes the administration's deployment planning into 1968 for Southeast Asia and other Pacific Command areas. It focuses especially on the impact of the planning on the Air Force's resources and world-wide defense posture.

Previous studies in this series are: USAF Plans and Operations in Southeast Asia, 1965; USAF Logistic Plans and Policies in Southeast Asia, 1965; USAF Plans and Policies in South Vietnam and Laos, 1964; and USAF Plans and Policies in South Vietnam, 1961-1963.

*Max Rosenberg*
MAX ROSENBERG
Chief
USAF Historical Division
 Liaison Office

# UNCLASSIFIED

# UNCLASSIFIED

## CONTENTS

FOREWORD

I. THE AIR FORCE VIEW OF SOUTHEAST ASIA STRATEGY . . . . . . . . . . 1

    The Limited U.S. Objectives . . . . . . . . . . . . . . . . . . . 2
    USAF Concern About the U.S. Buildup . . . . . . . . . . . . . . . 3
    The Decision to Resume Bombing of North Vietnam . . . . . . . . . . 6

II. INITIAL RESULTS OF 1966 DEPLOYMENT PLANNING . . . . . . . . . . . 10

    The Honolulu Conference of January-February . . . . . . . . . . . 10
    Reaction to the 1966 Requirements. . . . . . . . . . . . . . . . . 15
    Revised JCS-USAF Proposals and OSD's Guidelines . . . . . . . . . . 18

III. FURTHER USAF PLANNING . . . . . . . . . . . . . . . . . . . . . . 24

    McNamara's Decisions. . . . . . . . . . . . . . . . . . . . . . . 25
    Requirements for Thailand and Other PACOM Areas . . . . . . . . . 31
    Alignment of Air Munitions With Combat Sortie Needs . . . . . . . . 32
    Lagging Air Base Construction . . . . . . . . . . . . . . . . . . 35
    The War's Impact on Tactical Forces . . . . . . . . . . . . . . . 35
    OSD's 2 July Deployment Guidelines . . . . . . . . . . . . . . . . 36

IV. NEW ESTIMATES OF U.S. 1966-1967 DEPLOYMENT NEEDS . . . . . . . 38

    Admiral Sharp's Revised 1966 and 1967 Requirements. . . . . . . . . 39
    McNamara's Response . . . . . . . . . . . . . . . . . . . . . . . 41
    Air Force Study of Sharp's Additional Requirements . . . . . . . . . 45
    The Impact on the Air Force's World-Wide Posture . . . . . . . . . 50

V. YEAR-END DECISIONS . . . . . . . . . . . . . . . . . . . . . . . . 54

    The Honolulu Conference of October . . . . . . . . . . . . . . . . 54
    The Air Force-JCS Position on Sharp's 1966-1967 Needs . . . . . . . 58
    McNamara's Deployment Decisions . . . . . . . . . . . . . . . . . 63
    Air Force-JCS Reaction to McNamara's Decisions . . . . . . . . . . 67
    The Year-End Situation . . . . . . . . . . . . . . . . . . . . . . 70

NOTES . . . . . . . . . . . . . . . . . . . . . . . . . . . . . . . . . 75

GLOSSARY . . . . . . . . . . . . . . . . . . . . . . . . . . . . . . . 82

CHARTS . . . . . . . . . . . . . . . . . . . . . . . . . . . . . . . .

    1. Route Package Areas in North Vietnam . . . . . . . . . . . . . . 9
    2. PACAF Aircraft Deployment. . . . . . . . . . . . . . . . . . . . 71
    3. PACAF Aircraft Summary . . . . . . . . . . . . . . . . . . . . . 73

## UNCLASSIFIED

## I. THE AIR FORCE VIEW OF SOUTHEAST ASIA STRATEGY

(U) At the beginning of 1966 the American-South Vietnamese and allied military posture in Southeast Asia had improved over that of the previous year. The U.S. decision in 1965 to alter its mission from advice and support of the Republic of Vietnam (RVN) to open participation in air and ground combat had saved the Saigon government, now headed by Air Vice Marshal Nguyen Cao Ky, from certain defeat.

(S-Gp 3) Nevertheless, Viet Cong and North Vietnamese forces remained formidable adversaries. The strength of their regular and irregular units was estimated at about 265,100 personnel. Allied strength consisted of some 651,885 Vietnamese regular and paramilitary personnel and 184,314 American, 20,000 Korean, 1,500 Australian, and 100 New Zealand personnel. In neighboring Thailand U.S. strength stood at 14,107. Most of the U.S. air and ground units in South Vietnam and Thailand had arrived in the last half of 1965 in accordance with a "Phase I" deployment plan adopted in July of that year. Phase II deployments were about to begin.[1]

The USAF buildup had been rapid. In South Vietnam there were about 20,620 personnel and 514 aircraft and in Thailand 9,117 personnel and 207 aircraft. USAF tactical units in South Vietnam were assigned to and under the operational control of the 2d Air Division* at Tan Son Nhut AB, headed by Lt. Gen. Joseph H. Moore, Jr. In Thailand they were assigned to the 13th Air Force in the Philippines for administrative and logistic support and to the 2d Air Division for operations. In addition to USAF forces, there also had been a buildup of Navy, Marine Corps, and Army air units in Southeast Asia. Further, an impressive

---

* Effective 8 April 1966, the 2d Air Division was discontinued and Headquarters Seventh Air Force established.

array of backup air power, principally Air Force, was in position in the Philippines, Taiwan, Korea, Japan, Okinawa, and Guam. From Guam 30 B-52's, supported by KC-135 tankers based on Okinawa, since 18 June 1965 had engaged in interdiction and occasionally close support operations in South Vietnam.[2]

## The Limited U.S. Objectives

The basic American objective in Southeast Asia was to maintain an independent and non-communist Republic of Vietnam. This required destroying enemy forces by air and ground action in the South and selective interdiction of military targets in North Vietnam and Laos. The purpose of the interdiction program was to reduce the infiltration of men and supplies into South Vietnam, force the North Vietnamese to devote much of their efforts and resources to repair rail and road networks, and persuade them to come to the conference table. The Hanoi-Haiphong area and "buffer zones" near the Chinese border remained the principal "sanctuaries" against air attack. Other restraints on the use of air power also were imposed by the administration, which announced that it did not wish to destroy the North's political institutions nor precipitate a wider war. Its policy gave first priority to defeating the enemy with air, ground, and naval power in the South.[3]

(U) The deepening U.S. involvement in the war caused uneasiness in some sectors of American public opinion including the Congress. On 6 January a Senate subcommittee headed by Sen. Mike Mansfield, after a visit to the war theater, issued a troubled report. It declared that the entry of U.S. combat forces into the conflict had blunted but not turned back the Communist drive. The United States now faced, the report added, an "open-ended" military commitment of an ultimate size that could not be foreseen. The administration, however, did not waver in supporting its ally. From 6 to 8 February 1966 President Lyndon B. Johnson and Prime Minister Ky met in Honolulu to discuss the war, after which they issued a declaration reasserting their determination to resist aggression, search for a just and stable peace, and reconstruct the nation by constitutional, democratic means.[4]

## USAF Concern About the U.S. Buildup

test the willingness of the Hanoi regime to negotiate, the U.S. and Saigon governments in late 1965 had launched a major peace offensive. This included cessation on 24 December of USAF-Navy Rolling Thunder air strikes on the North, although the air and ground war in the South and Laos continued. Still in effect in January 1966, the bombing pause distressed the Joint Chiefs of Staff (JCS), especially the USAF Chief of Staff, Gen. John P. McConnell. He felt that the air strikes (begun on 7 February 1965) had been largely ineffective because of the political restraints imposed by the administration. Its policy exempted many important targets from air attack.[5]

Because of the administration's emphasis on the war in the South, there was a rising demand for more U.S. and allied ground forces. Following the accelerated 1965 deployments in accordance with Phase I planning, Adm. U.S. Grant Sharp, Commander-in-Chief, Pacific (CINCPAC), after coordinating with Gen. William Westmoreland, Commander, U.S. Military Assistance Command, Vietnam (COMUSMACV), sent to the JCS on 16 December 1965 "Phase II" and "Phase IIA" deployment plans. These called for a total of 486,500 U.S. and allied air and ground forces in South Vietnam and 169,000 in Thailand and other Pacific Command (PACOM) areas by the end of 1966. On 6 January 1966 McConnell warned Secretary of the Air Force Harold Brown that the support of such a large force would severely strain USAF resources, result in the withdrawal of sizeable air units from Europe, and transform most tactical fighter squadrons in the United States into training and rotation organizations. He foresaw a weakening of the visible U.S. deterrent around the periphery of Communist China and elsewhere in the world. He again urged (as had the JCS) federalizing national guard units, adding:

> In my evaluation of additional force requirements, I'm concerned not enough consideration is being given to the problem of greatest importance: the maintenance of a viable, flexible, and credible military posture measured against the worldwide Communist threat. The real threat to U.S. objectives and interest still remains China in the Western Pacific, and the USSR in Europe and against the continental United States. Therefore, while recognizing the immediacy and seriousness of the conflict in Southeast Asia, I believe we should view it in the perspective of the overall threat and examine alternate solutions and strategies to achieve our overall objectives.

urged adoption of a strategy based on the Concept of Vietnam paper approved by the JCS on 27 August 1965.* It postulated three major U.S. objectives of equal priority: force Hanoi to end its support to the Viet Cong; defeat the Viet Cong and extend control of the Saigon government over all of South Vietnam; deter the Chinese Communists and, if necessary, defeat them. He also advocated a continuous evaluation of the progress or lack of progress in the war to serve as a guide to future deployments.

important step in implementing this strategy, said McConnell, would be to end the bombing pause over North Vietnam "dramatically" and "forcefully." This act would strike at the heart of the insurgency, substitute U.S. technical superiority for a war of attrition, possibly shorten the war by months or years, and arrest a further imbalance in the U.S. military posture until the effects of the air campaign were known. He cited recent national intelligence estimates indicating that neither Hanoi nor Peking were likely to introduce substantial combat troops into the war as a result of intensified air

---

* See Jacob Van Staaveren, <u>USAF Plans and Operations in Southeast Asia, 1965,</u> (AFCHO, 1966), pp 90-99 (TS).

strikes. "I am therefore convinced," he concluded, "that before additional forces are deployed to Southeast Asia, serious consideration . . . be given to this proposal."[6]

Almost simultaneously McConnell joined the Marine Corps chief in asking the JCS to proceed with the task of making an evaluation of the progress of the war as a guide to determining the size of future U.S. deployments.[*][7]

Secretary Brown, in transmitting McConnell's views to Secretary of Defense Robert S. McNamara on 10 January, called them "revealing" and "challenging" and said they merited "serious consideration" before a final decision was made to increase American strength in Southeast Asia as Sharp recommended. He also submitted an initial analysis of the Air Force's manpower, aircraft, and ammunition resources, and of its training and field requirements to support the proposed 1966 buildup. He advised that USAF units and personnel were available but that the first quarter 1966 deployment schedule was unrealistic. He also cited numerous problems. There was a need to align requirements with capabilities, to resolve "lead time" for some units, and to obtain foreign country clearances to permit certain deployments. On 17 January he submitted to McNamara alternative ways for the Air Force to meet Sharp's needs during the year and to continue support of the war, if necessary, through fiscal year 1968.[8]

The Air Staff remained strongly opposed to the current military planning and strategy. On 24 January, during a JCS meeting with Deputy Secretary

---

[*] On 27 September 1965 McNamara asked the JCS to analyze the effects of U.S. ground operations in South Vietnam. On 10 November the JCS replied that it would make frequent evaluations to guide future operations and deployments. Progress was slow and the first one was not completed until 2 February 1966. However, the Air Force and the Marine Corps believed that the methodology and data needed more study. An approved evaluation was completed on 2 June.

of Defense Cyrus R. Vance, Gen. William H. Blanchard, USAF Vice Chief of Staff, reported that the Air Force had not approved Sharp's Phase II force proposals. He argued that without an evaluation of the present forces in South Vietnam and an intensified air war on the North, more U.S. forces could not be justified. But he was unsuccessful in reversing the deployment program which the Office of the Secretary of Defense (OSD) and the other services since late 1965 believed was necessary.[9]

## The Decision to Resume Bombing of North Vietnam

There was strong service support, however, for resuming and stepping up the air war against North Vietnam. On 8 January the Joint Chiefs informed McNamara that past experience, as in Korea, showed there was substantial risk in protracted negotiations during a "standdown" in air operations that could cost many American lives. They urged early resumption of air attacks to redress the advantages accruing to the North, to avoid Communist misinterpretation of U.S. resolve, and to insure that negotiations were from a position of strength. They suggested renewing the bombings 48 hours after a Soviet mission headed by Alexsander N. Shelepin, which was visiting Hanoi, returned to Moscow.* This was sufficient time for the Soviets to communicate to the United States any substantive results of their talks. The air strikes should exceed in scope and intensity those previously conducted. McNamara sent the recommendations to the State Department and replied on 19 January that the future of the Rolling Thunder was still under review.[10]

After another bombing analysis by the Central Intelligence Agency (CIA) and the Defense Intelligence Agency (DIA) confirmed that air strikes on the

---

\* The Shelepin mission was in Hanoi from 7 to 13 January.

economy and logistic system of North Vietnam had failed to reduce sufficiently the resupply of Communist forces in the South and Laos, the JCS again prepared an attack plan. Accepting McConnell's proposal, it agreed on 18 January that the bombing moratorium should end with a "sharp blow " and be followed up with expanded air operations throughout the North except for a 10-mile radius around Hanoi, Phuc Yen airfield, a 4-mile radius around Haiphong, and a 20-mile buffer zone near the Chinese border.* The Joint Chiefs also called for closing the principal seaports+ and removing other political restrictions against important targets. They cautioned that U.S. restraint might increase rather than decrease the danger of Chinese Communist intervention and result in a Communist and free world interpretation that it reflected American vacillation.[11]

A week later, having examined three alternate ways to resume the bombing, the Joint Chiefs agreed they should begin by attacks on all of the North's lines of communication and POL (petroleum, oil and lubricants) systems using USAF Thai-based and Navy carrier aircraft. This would be followed by air strikes on ferries, vehicles, pontoon bridges, and similar targets outside of the excluded areas. Admiral Sharp supported these and even heavier air attacks, believing it was the only way to bring Ho Chi Minh, the leader of North Vietnam, to the conference table.[12]

On 31 January, after receiving no satisfactory response from the Hanoi government to his peace effort, President Johnson ended the 37-day bombing moratorium and ordered the resumption of air strikes. They began the same day but not in accordance with JCS recommendations. Instead, the administration limited the attacks to armed reconnaissance, generally at the December 1965 level

---

\* This would reduce the "sanctuary" areas. See p 42.
+ The DIA estimated that in 1965, 67 percent of North Vietnam's imports arrived by sea, 33 percent by rail from China, and a negligible amount by road.

and continued to spare the Hanoi-Haiphong area. For the first two weeks the air strikes were restricted almost solely to "route package 1"* in southern North Vietnam where USAF and Navy aircraft struck targets on alternate days.[13]

As previously, the Joint Staff of the JCS without formal service participation planned Rolling Thunder operations in coordination with higher OSD and administration officials. Gen. Earle G. Wheeler, the JCS chairman, sent the Joint Chiefs the air programs submitted to McNamara for approval. He asked the services for a continuous review of target lists, for estimates on the frequency of air coverage needed to insure that certain facilities and routes remained out of action, and for advice on whether reconnaissance, air strikes, and targeting were commensurate with military effectiveness. Within the Air Staff, the Tactical Division, Directorate of Operations, monitored the air program against the North and kept McConnell and other USAF agencies fully informed. On 1 March a new series of Rolling Thunder attacks began which included some target areas outside of those in route package 1.[14]

---

* On 16 November 1965 Admiral Sharp divided North Vietnam into six "route packages" with specific "packages" assigned to the Air Force and the Navy. The Air Force's predominate area was in the northwest. Later, on 27 March, Admiral Sharp directed an adjustment whereby MACV was assigned operational control of route package 1 and authorized to interdict this area in conjunction with Tiger Hound operations in Laos.

# ROUTE PACKAGE AREAS
## NORTH VIETNAM
### 22 Apr 66

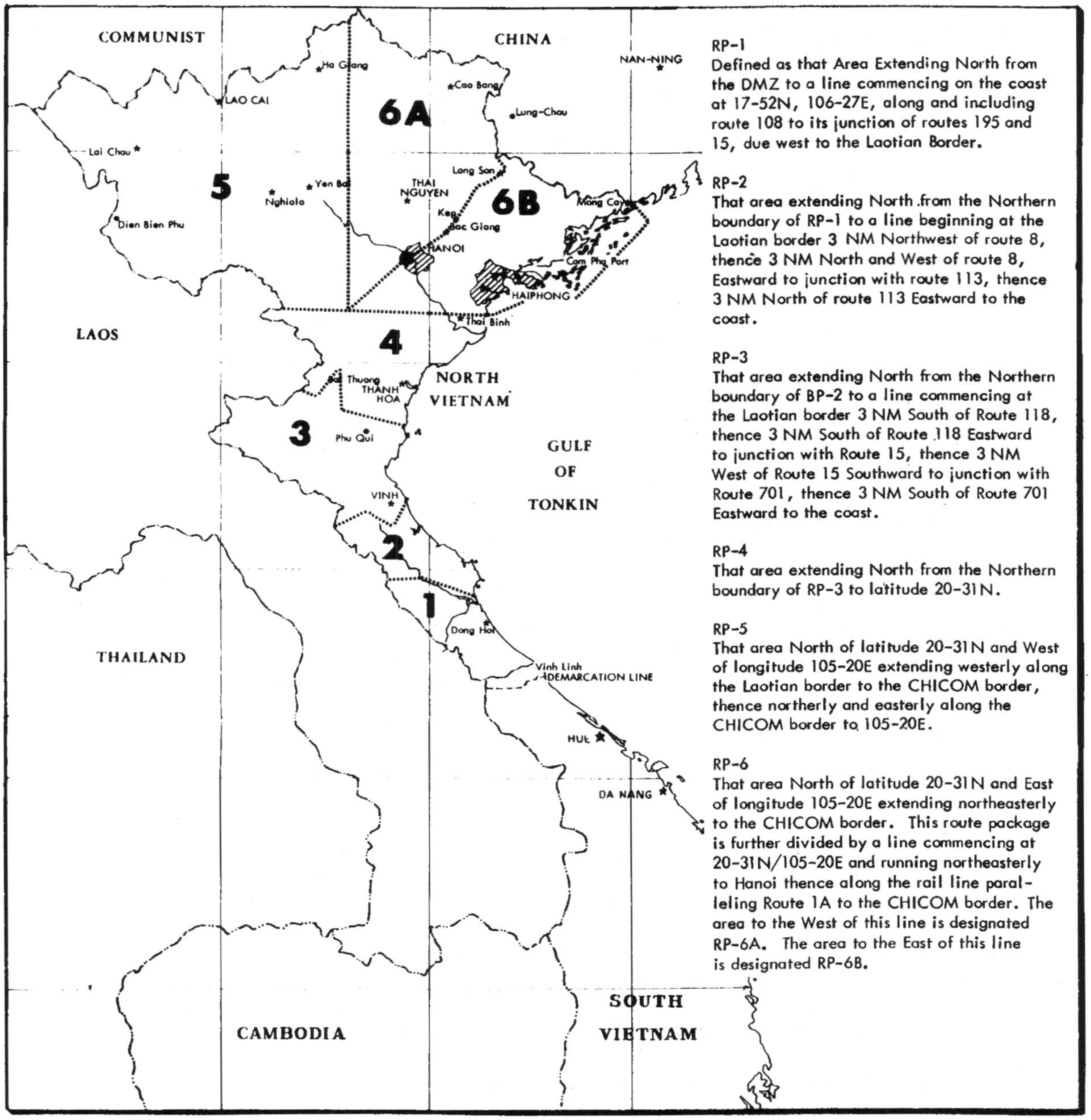

**RP-1**
Defined as that Area Extending North from the DMZ to a line commencing on the coast at 17-52N, 106-27E, along and including route 108 to its junction of routes 195 and 15, due west to the Laotian Border.

**RP-2**
That area extending North from the Northern boundary of RP-1 to a line beginning at the Laotian border 3 NM Northwest of route 8, thence 3 NM North and West of route 8, Eastward to junction with route 113, thence 3 NM North of route 113 Eastward to the coast.

**RP-3**
That area extending North from the Northern boundary of BP-2 to a line commencing at the Laotian border 3 NM South of Route 118, thence 3 NM South of Route 118 Eastward to junction with Route 15, thence 3 NM West of Route 15 Southward to junction with Route 701, thence 3 NM South of Route 701 Eastward to the coast.

**RP-4**
That area extending North from the Northern boundary of RP-3 to latitude 20-31N.

**RP-5**
That area North of latitude 20-31N and West of longitude 105-20E extending westerly along the Laotian border to the CHICOM border, thence northerly and easterly along the CHICOM border to 105-20E.

**RP-6**
That area North of latitude 20-31N and East of longitude 105-20E extending northeasterly to the CHICOM border. This route package is further divided by a line commencing at 20-31N/105-20E and running northeasterly to Hanoi thence along the rail line paralleling Route 1A to the CHICOM border. The area to the West of this line is designated RP-6A. The area to the East of this line is designated RP-6B.

Source: USAF Mgt Summary, 22 Apr 66

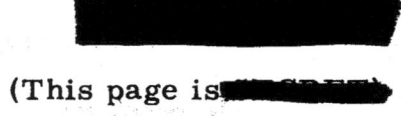

## II. INITIAL RESULTS OF 1966 DEPLOYMENT PLANNING

(U) Even while the bombing pause continued, the Air Force and the other services were studying new proposals to increase substantially U.S. and allied forces in Southeast Asia. On 17 January Sharp convened a conference at Honolulu to examine unit and manpower deployment goals and to draft a schedule. The conference lasted three weeks. Secretary McNamara attended the closing days and was briefed on all aspects of the war including the status of service deployment planning.

### The Honolulu Conference of January-February

In reviewing the air war, Pacific Command (PACOM) briefers reported that in 1965 the initial USAF and Navy Rolling Thunder attacks on North Vietnam had caused much confusion in that country. But the people soon recovered and devised elaborate repair techniques, built rail and road by-passes and underwater causeways, used fords, ferries, and human portage, practiced camouflage and other deception, shuttled goods from rails to roads to waterways, traveled at night, and dispersed supplies to isolated locations. They employed many "old tricks" used in the Korean War. This was possible because Rolling Thunder was a highly selective air program with many important targets exempt from attack or not heavily bombed.

For the months ahead CINCPAC plans called for more sorties each month against the North to suppress antiaircraft fire and for armed reconnaissance, combat air patrol (against MIG's), escort, and "recap." About 60 percent of these sorties would concentrate on hitting rail, road, and associated targets to reduce the overland flow of supplies through the Hanoi-Haiphong area; about 30 percent against lines of communication south of Hanoi and Haiphong; and 10 percent against key port and high-value targets in the Hanoi-Haiphong region.

In Laos the allocation of more USAF-Navy sorties would consist of about 65 percent for fixed targets, 20 percent for day and night reconnaissance of roads and trails, and 15 percent to satisfy "on-call" requests under "Bango" or "Whiplash"* procedures and to provide some air support, using USAF forward air controllers (FAC's), for the Lao Army in its struggle against the Communist-led Pathet Lao. More sorties probably would be allocated to the Tiger Hound program in southern Laos as the air effort there became more effective. In both Laos and North Vietnam additional USAF-Navy reconnaissance flights would seek out more targets.

As a measure of the air task in South Vietnam, Communist strength was estimated at 98 Viet Cong and 31 North Vietnam main force battalions (108 confirmed, 10 probable, and 11 possible). According to DIA estimates, these forces required less than 100 tons of supplies per day from outside the country but by December 1966, when their strength was expected to be 172 battalions (despite 70,000 casualties anticipated during the year), they would need 150 tons per day from North Vietnam. Thus the U.S. and allied objective was to reduce this tonnage and cut infiltration below the current rate of 4,500 personnel per month+ and this would require many more aircraft.

Admiral Sharp expected his proposed stepped-up air campaign against Communist external aid to have little immediate effect. After the North's POL system was destroyed, he thought Hanoi would establish a coastal supply system, a major task, and devise other new measures to maintain logistic support. He also predicted a greater shipping effort by China.

---

* Code names for special alert USAF attack and reconnaissance aircraft stationed in Thailand to insure fast strikes on targets of opportunity in Laos.
+ See p 39

Sharp felt there was a clear need for much more manpower in South Vietnam. He explained how the overall estimates of air, ground, and naval strength had risen through four recent planning stages: Phase I, 220,000; Phase II, 112,400; Phase IIA, 57,500; and Phase IIA (revised), 68,900. This would place about 459,000 U.S. military personnel in South Vietnam at the end of 1966 and there would be a requirement for 45,000 other allied troops or a total of 504,000. Subtracting the 195,414 U.S. and allied forces (184,314 U.S. and 21,100 allied) already in the South at the end of 1965, a total of 274,700 U.S. and 23,900 allied (Korean, Australian, and New Zealand) personnel had to be deployed during the year. U.S. Forces in Thailand and other PACOM areas would reach 172,000 personnel in the same period.

Sharp presented three alternate ways or "cases" for calculating Air Force, Army, and Navy personnel resources to meet his requirements. They were defined as follows:

Case I. The current U.S. force structure plus an increase in the active force structure; a feasible "drawdown" from oversea areas; call-up of selected reserve units and individuals; and extension of terms of service.

Case II. The current U.S. force structure plus an increase in the active force structure and a feasible "drawdown" from oversea areas.

Case III. The current U.S. force structure plus an increase in the active force structure.

Using his projected December 1966 estimate as a "base line" (459,000 U.S. personnel in Vietnam) for calculating service manpower needs, Sharp indicated how close to the goal he could come in each case:

|  | Case I | | Case II | | Case III | |
| --- | --- | --- | --- | --- | --- | --- |
|  | Pro-grammed | Short-fall | Pro-grammed | Short-fall | Pro-grammed | Short-fall |
| Air Force | 52,000 |  | 50,000 | 2,000 | 46,000 | 6,000 |
| Navy | 30,000 |  | 25,000 | 5,000 | 22,000 | 8,000 |
| Marine Corps | 70,000 |  | 70,000 |  | 70,000 |  |
| Army | 277,000 | 30,000 | 254,000 | 53,000 | 197,000 | 119,000 |
| Total | 429,000 | 30,000 | 399,000 | 60,000 | 335,000 | 133,000 |

The figures showed that under the most advantageous manpower policies that might be adopted--as in Case I--there would still be a shortage of 30,000 Army personnel at the end of 1966. This would prevent the deployment of sufficient troops to form a total of 122 "maneuver" battalions (102 for South Vietnam, 20 for the PACOM reserve) that he desired.

The Air Force, Navy, and Marine Corps indicated they could fulfill Sharp's air power requests during the year under Case I manpower policies. However, an examination of air ammunition stocks for the remainder of 1966 showed that only 648,000 tons would be available against a requirement for 700,000 tons. Taking into account this limitation, PACOM and MACV planners calculated air sortie requirements as follows:

| Sorties | Use |
| --- | --- |
| 150 per month per maneuver battalion | For U.S.-free world forces in South Vietnam |
| 7,800 per month | For support of Vietnamese forces |
| 3,000 per month | For Laos |
| 7,100 per month | For North Vietnam |

To support this schedule and maintain the U.S. air posture, it was estimated that in addition to Navy air units, tactical fighter strength by the end of the year should consist of 18 USAF and 10 Marine Corps squadrons in South Vietnam and 11 USAF squadrons in Thailand. The planners also proposed to increase B-52 (Arc Light) monthly sortie to 400 in February, 450 from April through June, and 600 from July through December. Five B-52 sorties per month would be flown with BLU-3B bomblets.

In reply to several questions raised by McNamara on the use of air power, PACOM briefers expressed the opinion that: (1) an air campaign limited to lines of communication in North Vietnam and Laos probably would not degrade significantly the North's capability to support the war in 1966 but would reduce it somewhat by mid-1967; (2) striking harbors, rail lines, thermal power plants, POL, and other high-value targets in addition to lines of communication would have little effect in the first half of 1966 but would have a significant impact in 1967; (3) striking North Vietnam's air bases would not prompt the Chinese to enter the war but the bases should not be hit until the MIG's began to interfere with air operations.*

Sharp observed that despite increased air and ground deployments the war promised to be a long one. There was uncertainty about service ability to meet his program and there would be major dificulties in providing adequate port facilities to handle the accelerated troop buildup.

Sharp sent the results of the conference to the JCS on 12 February. A separate report from Headquarters Pacific Air Forces (PACAF) to the Air Staff indicated that the three-case evaluation for South Vietnam had been prepared by Westmoreland's staff and for North Vietnam and Laos by Sharp's staff with little or no "input" by the component services. The evaluations were described as a

---

* Except for attacks on North Vietnam's airfields at Vinh in May 1965 and Dong Hoi in June 1965, the administration prohibited strikes on the North's airfields despite 11 recommendations submitted by McConnell or the JCS between 18 November 1964 and 18 January 1966 that this be done.

"purely mathematical development of the effectiveness of the United States and free world forces" against the Communist forces. Given only a day and a half to comment, Headquarters PACAF had not had sufficient time to examine in detail the data, the "ground rules" for the Case I, II, and III deployments, or the recommendations. Generally, PACAF was more optimistic about the expected effect of the proposed air campaign and it stressed the importance of the interrelationship of operations in South Vietnam, North Vietnam, and Laos in any assessment of the war's progress.[1]

## Reaction to the 1966 Requirements

After his return to Washington, McNamara reviewed the results of the Honolulu conference with the service secretaries, the JCS, and OSD officials. He directed that deployment planning be based on Case I requirements--but not on the manpower policies that had been proposed. He specifically rejected, in accordance with current policy, any call-up of reserve forces or extension of terms of service. He advised that a final decision on the ultimate manpower goal would be made after further service studies. The Defense Secretary and some other administration officials were not overoptimistic. They thought upwards of 600,000 or more men might be needed to reduce significantly the level of conflict but this size force raised the spectre of Chinese Communist intervention. The officials agreed that the Chinese probably would intervene to prevent a defeat of the North but the chances were only "a little better than even" that they would not intervene to save the South, at least for the time being.[2]

McNamara's order set in motion a major service planning and data assembling effort. To guide it, OSD established a Southeast Asia Program Team chaired by Dr. Victor K. Heyman--thus by-passing the JCS. The team began preparing additional deployment tables containing all essential information on

available military aircraft, logistic, construction, manpower, and other resources. Each service was asked to establish counterpart teams. Maj. Gen. John D. Lavelle, Director of Aerospace Programs, Headquarters USAF, headed the Air Force team that included representatives from all key Air Staff offices. In a separate action, at the request of Secretary Brown and General McConnell, the Air Staff also created an ad hoc study group* under Col. Leroy J. Manor of the Directorate of Operations. The group was assigned the task of scrutinizing Sharp's tactical air proposals for Southeast Asia. The Operations directorate also conducted "Exercise 68A," an analysis of the Air Force's tactical fighter structure.[3]

Meanwhile, on 21 February, after reviewing Admiral Sharp's documents, General McConnell and the other members of the JCS agreed to proceed with planning to send the military forces in accordance with tentative time tables or as soon as possible thereafter. Major USAF units scheduled for deployment in 1966 were as follows:[4]

| Aircraft | South Vietnam | Thailand |
|---|---|---|
| Tactical fighters* | 10 sqs | 6 sqs |
| C-130's |  | 2 sqs |
| RF-101's | 4 a/c |  |
| RF-4C's | 1 sq | 14 a/c |
| B-66B's |  | 8 a/c |
| RB-66C's |  | 13 a/c |
| O-1's | 68 a/c |  |
| **Other Units** | | |
| Tactical control party | 1+ | |
| Airborne battlefield command and control center | 1 | 1 |
| Heavy repair units | 3 | 1 |

* This group subsequently expanded and on 15 July 1966 became the Operations Review Group within the Directorate of Operations.
+ 122 personnel.

The Air Staff still believed, however, that the strategy of "matching" enemy manpower was wrong and that the proper use of air and naval power would make unnecessary most of the proposed forces. It foresaw many problems such as insufficient air munitions until the third quarter of fiscal year 1967 and delays in air base construction with consequent slippages in deployments. It felt that no air units should be sent until they could be supported effectively and that some Air National Guard (ANG) units would be needed to minimize the "drawdown" that threatened the posture of the U.S. Air Forces in Europe (USAFE). If OSD decided to proceed with the Case I plan, the Air Force could meet its commitments only at the cost of withdrawing most reconnaissance aircraft from Europe, using substantially more Tactical Air Command (TAC) fighter squadrons, and diverting many USAF personnel from bases around the globe.[5]

The Air Staff's review of air bases and facilities was especially discouraging. Slippages already loomed in readying the six air bases (four in South Vietnam, two in Thailand) approved or under construction at the end of 1965.* Work was initiated in 1965 on only three of the bases, Cam Ranh Bay and Phan Rang in South Vietnam and Sattahip in Thailand, and only Cam Ranh Bay had an emergency air strip at the start of 1966. No work had begun at Tuy Hoa in South Vietnam and two sites, one each in South Vietnam and Thailand, remained to be designated.

At the January-February Honolulu conference, Tuy Hoa was tentatively dropped in favor of a site near Qui Nhon (later Phu Cat AB), and the need for two more sites, still undesignated, was reaffirmed. In anticipation of still greater air requirements, the Air Force pressed for another new base, but Sharp thought it was desirable rather than necessary. To acquire new bases and facilities,

---

* See Herman S. Wolk, USAF Logistic Plans and Policies in Southeast Asia 1965, (TS), (AFCHO, 1967).

the Air Force depended primarily on the Army and Navy but their construction units were concentrating on building ports and supply depots. As an alternative, the Air Staff studied the feasibility of employing an independent contractor to do some of the Air Force's construction.[6]

Meanwhile, McNamara had sent tentative Case I deployment schedules to the service secretaries and asked how they proposed to meet them. He urged they exercise "all ingenuity possible." Secretary Brown, on 19 February, requested quick approval to allow the Air Force to dispatch two F-100 squadrons to Spain in permanent change of station (PCS) status in place of three squadrons currently rotating to Turkey on temporary duty (TDY); retain a MACE wing, scheduled for withdrawal, in USAFE for the duration of the war in Southeast Asia; convert the "Skoshi Tiger" F-5 squadron (11 UE), which was undergoing evaluation in South Vietnam, to a complete squadron (18 UE) to form one of the 16 additional USAF fighter units needed in 1966; assign two more F-102 PCS squadrons to Southeast Asia; and convert one F-102 squadron in Okinawa to PCS status. To support the deployment plan, the Air Staff also estimated that 81 more O-1's were needed through fiscal year 1967 and requested the immediate transfer of this number from the Army.[7]

## Revised JCS-USAF Proposals and OSD's Guidelines

The results of the Air Staff's exercises and preliminary analysis of its capabilities were sent to the Joint Staff in late February. On 1 March, after further study of Case I needs, the JCS recommended to McNamara that he approve Sharp's force requests but that deployments be extended over a 16-month rather than a 10-month period (i.e., by the end of June 1967). Even with maximum effort, it said, all military units would not be available by the end of 1966. To attempt to send them would unbalance combat and support elements and excessive withdrawal of units from Europe and the Atlantic Command would entail too much risk.

As a substitute for Sharp's operational plan, the JCS recommended adoption of the Concept of Vietnam paper which had been approved by the JCS on 27 August and modified on 10 November 1965. In addition to bringing more pressure on the Communists in South Vietnam, this document called for strikes on the North's war-supporting industries in the Hanoi-Haiphong area, aerial mining of ports, extensive interdiction of inland and coastal waterways, and more special air and ground operations in Laos. Infiltration was to be made as costly as possible.

Because of OSD's strictures against calling up reserve forces or extending terms of service, the JCS scaled downward the proposed deployments. Case I capabilities for South Vietnam by the end of 1966 were now placed at 413,557 U.S. personnel but the service chiefs recommended a goal of 377,849. They also proposed 37,700 U.S. personnel for Thailand. As part of the reduction the Air Force would stretch out the deployment of tactical fighter squadrons, sending 12 rather than 16 to the two countries by year's end. The other four squadrons would be sent in the first half of 1967. World-wide adjustments would include reducing USAFE's tactical fighter strength from 21 to 20 squadrons and tactical reconnaissance strength from 9 to 5 squadrons. [8]

Separate papers addressed the problems of logistics, withdrawals from Europe, reserve units, the war reserve, the military assistance programs, air munitions, air base construction, and South Vietnamese capabilities. [9]

Each service also replied individually to McNamara. Secretary Brown reported on 3 March that Air Staff analysis of the impact of the Case I program showed that while all 16 USAF fighter squadrons could be sent in 1966-- assuming beyond the most optimistic hopes that there would be sufficient airfields-- the Air Force would still need to use some reserve personnel to maintain an adequate training base. He also cited other important USAF requirements in addition to those he had enumerated on 19 February. They included: providing sufficient F-5 production to equip the special air warfare force; transferring remaining USAF A-1 aircraft (being reduced in numbers because of attrition and because they were out of production) to the Vietnamese Air Force (VNAF); reducing sortie rates and controlling munitions expenditures because of the growing air munitions shortage; increasing aircraft production regardless of whether the war ended in fiscal year 1967 or continued into 1968; increasing the Air Force's manpower ceiling for fiscal year 1966 to assure retention of experienced airmen and to fill the procurement training "pipeline" for fiscal year 1967; and procuring 35 more airborne radio direction finding (ARDF) C-47's "Hawkeye" aircraft to fix each week the location of 1,200 enemy stations. The latter action would obviate the need to obtain more Army U-6 and U-8 aircraft for this purpose.

Brown further reiterated the need for action to raise the skill level of weapon and munition handlers and return to "cockpits" pilots holding staff and support positions and to fill the vacated chairs. There also was a concurrent need to step up tactical fighter pilot training and to take steps to forestall a shortage of air liaison officer and forward air control (ALO/FAC) personnel. He especially stressed the need to maintain an adequate USAF training and resources base and to prepare for the "long pull," if necessary, into fiscal year 1968.

With respect to further deployment adjustments, Brown recommended the transfer of four squadrons from USAFE with three of them (2 RF-4C's and 1 B/RB-66) going to Southeast Asia and one (B/RB-66) to the United States for use in tactical training. He also recommended the withdrawal and transfer of five PACAF tactical fighter squadrons from special integrated operational planning (SIOP) quick-reaction status to Southeast Asia. Finally, he proposed that Admiral Sharp's sortie requirements be fulfilled on the basis of sortie capability rather than by the numbers of aircraft deployed.[10]

 10 March, after reviewing the submissions of the JCS and service secretaries, McNamara advised them that their recommendations required more study. Pending further notice, he directed that deployments to Southeast Asia be carried out in accordance with Case I guidelines as contained in OSD-prepared tables. He reaffirmed the need to meet manpower goals without calling up reserves or extending terms of military service. In deploying units McNamara asked the Joint Chiefs to eliminate any schedule "slippages" as soon as feasible, request where necessary deployment change proposals, and submit new deployment tables compatible with the ones prepared by OSD. The latter included actual and projected troop deployments in the plan of 11 December 1965.* The Defense Secretary assigned to OSD's Southeast Asia Program Division the responsibility for developing more formats, maintaining deployment data, showing reasons for deployment slippages, and expediting actions. The initial tables showed the following manpower and aircraft goals for Southeast Asia and contained the latest statistical revisions made by the JCS and the services:[11]

### Total U.S. Strength in South Vietnam

|  | Dec 65 | Jun 66 | Dec 66 | Jun 67 |
|---|---|---|---|---|
| Dec 65 Plan | 194,500 | 277,800 | 367,800 | 393,900 |
| Case I Capabilities |  | 283,500 | 415,000 | 425,600 |
| Service Capabilities |  | 290,700 | 394,800 | 427,900 |
| JCS Recommendations | 179,100 | 288,100 | 374,200 | 411,100 |

### Total USAF Strength in South Vietnam

|  | Dec 65 | Jun 66 | Dec 66 | Jun 67 |
|---|---|---|---|---|
| Dec 65 Plan | 28,200 | 38,000 | 43,600 | 43,600 |
| Case I Capabilities |  | 40,000 | 47,300 | 47,300 |
| Service Capabilities |  | 38,600 | 48,300 | 53,600 |
| JCS Recommendations | 20,600 | 38,600 | 47,900 | 52,400 |

* This "base line" plan represented the Presidential request for the fiscal year 1966 supplemental appropriation for Southeast Asia.

### Total U.S. Strength in Thailand

|  | Dec 65 | Jun 66 | Dec 66 | Jun 67 |
|---|---|---|---|---|
| Dec 65 Plan | 16,700 | 22,700 | 26,800 | 28,400 |
| Case I Capabilities |  | 28,100 | 44,400 | 49,100 |
| Service Capabilities |  | 25,200 | 37,700 | 46,200 |
| JCS Recommendations | 13,900 | 25,200 | 37,700 | 46,200 |

### Total USAF Strength in Thailand

|  | Dec 65 | Jun 66 | Dec 66 | Jun 67 |
|---|---|---|---|---|
| Dec 65 Plan | 11,600 | 14,700 | 16,900 | 16,900 |
| Case I Capabilities |  | 20,600 | 31,200 | 31,200 |
| Service Capabilities |  | 17,700 | 28,300 | 28,300 |
| JCS Recommendations | 9,100 | 17,700 | 28,300 | 28,300 |

### Total U.S. Attack Capable Aircraft

|  | Dec 65 | Jun 66 | Dec 66 | Jun 67 |
|---|---|---|---|---|
| Dec 65 Plan | 711 | 789 | 918 | 917 |
| Case I Capabilities |  | 866 | 1,087 | 1,081 |
| Service Capabilities |  | 877 | 1,015 | 1,091 |
| JCS Recommendations | 681 | 877 | 1,015 | 1,081 |

### Total USAF Attack Capable Aircraft *

|  | Dec 65 | Jun 66 | Dec 66 | Jun 67 |
|---|---|---|---|---|
| Dec 65 Plan | 398 | 446 | 590 | 590 |
| Case I Capabilities |  | 536 | 716 | 716 |
| Service Capabilities |  | 547 | 644 | 716 |
| JCS Recommendations | 380 | 547 | 644 | 716 |

### Total U.S. Non-Attack Aircraft

|  | Dec 65 | Jun 66 | Dec 66 | Jun 67 |
|---|---|---|---|---|
| Dec 65 Plan | 829 | 898 | 964 | 976 |
| Case I Capabilities |  | 1,042 | 1,292 | 1,326 |
| Service Capabilities |  | 1,009 | 1,250 | 1,333 |
| JCS Recommendations | 770 |  |  |  |

### Total USAF Non-Attack Aircraft +

|  | Dec 65 | Jun 66 | Dec 66 | Jun 67 |
|---|---|---|---|---|
| Dec 65 Plan | 401 | 422 | 464 | 464 |
| Case I Capabilities |  | 570 | 721 | 716 |
| Service Capabilities |  | 537 | 741 | 776 |
| JCS Recommendations | 1,367 | 537 | 721 | 716 |

---

* Defined as A-1, T-28, B-57, F-4, F-5, F-100, F-104, and F-105.
+ Defined as RB-57, B/RB-66, RF-4, RF-101, F-102, FC-47, C-47, C-54, RC-47, EC-121, and C-123.

Similar compilations were made of U.S. helicopter strength. The December 1965 Plan called for 1,466. Case I capabilities by June 1967 required 2,428 against service capabilities of 1,819. USAF capability by that date was placed at 78.

## III. FURTHER USAF PLANNING

Following issuance of McNamara's 10 March guidelines, the Air Force began an intensive planning effort to prepare for and ease the impact of Phase II deployment on its world-wide personnel and other resources. With the rate of first-term Air Force reenlistments at the lowest point in history, the retention of skilled airmen was recognized as an especially critical problem. In this regard, on 11 March Under Secretary of the Air Force Norman S. Paul emphasized to OSD the importance of stabilizing the variable reenlistment program and increasing proficiency pay. He also asked for an additional 33,416 military and 2,426 civilian spaces for fiscal year 1966 and 52,022 military and 12,380 civilian spaces for fiscal year 1967.[1]

Air bases in theater constituted another major problem area. A base survey made by Lt. Gen. Glen W. Martin, the USAF Inspector General, disclosed that crowding on existing bases such as Tan Son Nhut* was about twice that experienced in the Korean War. The congestion was certain to increase because of accelerated unit deployments and delays in completing the six new air bases approved in 1965.+ [2]

Sites for two of the bases were not determined until after the beginning of 1966: on 23 February for Nam Phong AB near Khon Kaen, Thailand, and on 1 March for Phu Cat AB near Qui Nhon. Because of slippages in the building program, McConnell urged the JCS to provide sufficient construction assistance to the Air Force to meet beneficial occupancy dates (BOD's). On 19 March Secretary Brown recommended to McNamara that the Air Force be authorized to build Tuy Hoa AB using a civilian construction firm and a cost-plus-fixed-fee contract. He desired to construct Phu Cat AB in the same manner if access could

---
\* General Martin reported that there were nearly 570 USAF, 412 Army and Navy, and 350 VNAF aircraft and helicopters on six primary bases in South Vietnam. These figures did not include transient aircraft.
+ See p 17.

be provided outside of the congested port of Qui Nhon.  In addition, he considered essential another air base in the northern part of the I Corps area.³

On 21 March Brown sent McNamara the Air Force's preferred unit deployment schedule from May through November 1966 for Southeast Asia and other PACOM areas.  It provided for the retention in South Vietnam of a full unit-equipped F-5 Skoshi Tiger squadron; the transfer of certain F-100, F-102, F-104, F-105, and F-4C squadrons from the United States to South Vietnam, Thailand, and Japan; and the transfer of similar tactical squadrons from Japan, Okinawa and the Philippines to South Vietnam and Thailand.  The USAF plan would require some withdrawal of units from USAFE, principally four F-4C squadrons and 64 reconnaissance-type aircraft, many equipped for electronic countermeasures or intelligence, for use in the war zone.  The F-4C squadrons would deploy to Thailand in October and November for six months TDY.  He asked for immediate decisions on squadron withdrawals and adjustments in USAFE and on procuring more F-5 aircraft.

Secretary Brown also requested authority to place similar-type aircraft on the same bases to simplify logistic support and asked OSD to arrange for foreign country "clearances" to permit the recommended squadron transfers.  He restated USAF's requirement for about 33,000 and 52,000 additional USAF military personnel for fiscal years 1966 and 1967, respectively.⁴

## McNamara's Decisions

On 26 March McNamara sent the services his approved Case I combat sortie and tactical aircraft requirements.  His sortie figures (again prepared by OSD's Southeast Asia Program Division) were as follows:

|  | Jan 66* | Jun 66 | Dec 66 | Year-end Total |
|---|---|---|---|---|
| South Vietnam | 15,390 | 18,490 | 24,290 | 231,780 |
| North Vietnam |  | 7,407 + | 7,407 + | 81,477 |
| Laos | 3,000 | 3,000 | 3,000 | 36,000 |
| Total | 18,390 | 28,897 | 34,697 | 349,257 |

In a refinement of Sharp's proposals, sorties in South Vietnam were so distributed as to insure 150 per month for U.S., Korean, and Australian Army battalions and 200 per month for U.S. and Korean Marine battalions. About 7,800 sorties per month, as previously estimated, were allocated to Vietnamese ground forces. The greatest air effort would continue to be made in South Vietnam in accordance with established priorities. A major conclusion of OSD's analysis of combat air needs was that five fewer USAF tactical fighter squadrons were needed; that is, 11 rather than 16 squadrons as proposed by Sharp. Accordingly, McNamara deferred the deployment of three squadrons tentatively scheduled for South Vietnam and two for Thailand. He made no change in U.S. Navy or Marine Corps fighter strength. Thus, U.S. and VNAF tactical combat aircraft in the theater would consist of:

|  | Jan 66 ++ | Jun 66 | Dec 66 |
|---|---|---|---|
| USAF # | 355 | 463 | 614 |
| USN (3 CVA's) | 209 | 194 | 204 |
| USMC | 125 | 140 | 167 |
| VNAF | 125 | 150 | 150 |
| Total | 814 | 947 | 1,135 |

McNamara emphasized the importance of meeting Case I goals as efficiently as possible. He cautioned the services against deploying more aircraft than necessary, stating that the number could be increased if experience showed this to be essential.[5]

---

\* Actual sorties flown.
\+ About 5,185 sorties would be actual attack sorties.
++ Actual aircraft.
\# USAF aircraft were defined as A-1, B-57, F-100, F-104, F-5, F-4, and F-105. Excluded were T-28's, F-102's and B-52's.

Both the Air Staff and Sharp objected to the deferral of the five USAF squadrons. The Air Staff justified them on the basis of supporting CINCPAC's concept of operations. If the concept was not going to be followed, as appeared likely, more rather than fewer combat sorties were needed to hit fleeting targets. McConnell and the service chiefs officially protested, informing the Defense Secretary that the five squadrons would provide a 7- to 10- percent "margin" capability for unforeseen air demands, for surges in combat tempo, for the support of more Tiger Hound, Cricket,* and cross-border operations in Laos, and for attacks on more targets as they were uncovered.[6]

McNamara was unswayed by these arguments. Meanwhile, he made several other major decisions. On 25 March, as a result of France's recent decision to withdraw from the North Atlantic Treaty Organization (NATO),+ he ordered all USAFE reconnaissance squadrons out of France. Two would go to England to release two others there for South Vietnam and four would return to the United States. He approved substituting three PCS tactical fighter squadrons in Spain for three on TDY and the temporary reduction of U.S. Army forces in Europe from 225,000 to 207,000 by August 1966. After this date Army strength would rise again. He advised that there should be no change or any significant reduction in U.S. combat capability in Europe because of South Vietnam except as forced on the United States by the French President, Charles de Gaulle.[7]

At the end of March McNamara approved many of Secretary Brown's unit deployment recommendations. These included the transfer of seven B-66B aircraft from Europe to Southeast Asia and the formation of a F-5 squadron using the Skoshi Tiger unit as the nucleus. He also approved the deployment from the

---
* Tiger Hound and Cricket were special air programs in Laos.
+ Announced on 21 Feb 66 by President Charles de Gaulle.

United States or from a PACAF area outside of Southeast Asia of one F-100 squadron to South Vietnam and one F-105 squadron and four RF-101 aircraft to Thailand, one F-4C squadron from South Vietnam to Thailand, one F-102 and one F-104 squadrons from the United States to South Vietnam (for air defense), and four RF-101 aircraft from France to Southeast Asia.

The Defense Secretary agreed to permit the Air Force to replace individual aircraft in Southeast Asia on a "one for one" basis using resources in PACAF or the United States. He wished to review further the Air Force's recommendation to replace three F-100 TDY squadrons in Turkey with two F-100 PCS squadrons in Spain, to reprogram funds to increase F-5 production because of A-1 attrition, and to deploy aircraft on the basis of sorties. The latter proposal required a JCS evaluation.[8]

With respect to manpower requests, in March OSD funding actions allowed an increase in the variable reenlistment bonus and certain incremental increases in the overall USAF military and civilian personnel ceiling. It took no immediate steps to boost proficiency pay.[9]

Meanwhile, the Joint Chiefs, on the basis of McNamara's interim guidance of 10 March, completed an integrated deployment plan which they forwarded to OSD on 4 April. For South Vietnam they proposed a minor change, a buildup to 376,350 U.S. personnel* at the end of 1966 and 438,207 at the end of 1967. Other free world (i.e., non-Vietnamese) forces would total 45,047 for both years. For Thailand they proposed a major decrease--to 24,425 personnel for the end of 1966 and 33,347 for the end of 1967--plus additional personnel for other PACOM areas.

The JCS subsequently explained that its recommendations reflected the absence of any firm OSD manpower decisions in February, and the

---
* See p 21.

continued prohibition against calling up reserve forces or extending terms of service. Even with "extraordinary effort," it declared, there was no way to overcome certain shortages of military skills. Another factor cited was that the revised manpower goals of the Case I plan of 10 March would deploy existing units whereas the JCS plan called for activating new ones.

By the end of 1966 the latter plan would provide 70 U.S. and 23 allied maneuver battalions, other supporting engineer, field artillery, and air defense battalions, 33 USAF and Marine Corps tactical squadrons, and 75 helicopter companies and squadrons. USAF deployments from April through August would add 11 more fighter squadrons (6 F-101, 1 F-5, 1 F-102, 1 F-104, and 2 undetermined), one RF-4C squadron, and four RF-101 aircraft. The JCS again urged the deployment of the five USAF squadrons deferred on 10 March.[10]

In response to an Air Staff request, CINCPAC recomputed his combat sortie needs and the results were sent to McNamara on 15 April. Sharp now reported that North Vietnam and Laos required 12,407 sorties per month compared with 10,407 approved by McNamara on 26 March.* The increase was attributed to greater logistic dispersal by the North Vietnamese, the need for more armed reconnaissance, and weather problems. An air sortie deficit loomed beginning January 1967 but it could be overcome by deploying three of the five deferred squadrons to Thailand. The two other squadrons, if deployed to South Vietnam, would assure more flexibility in the use of air power. The Air Staff position was that the five squadrons should be deployed early in 1967 and steps taken to provide adequate basing.[11]

Except for the five deferred USAF squadrons and some other units, McNamara approved on 11 April most of the JCS integrated deployment plan through June 1967. He withheld comment on all manpower needs in Thailand and

---
* See p 26.

other PACOM areas pending another JCS study. The force structure, as reworked by OSD's Southeast Asia Programs Division, was as follows:[12]

### U.S. Military Strength in South Vietnam

|  | Dec 65* | Mar 66* | Jun 66 | Dec 66 | Jun 67 |
|---|---|---|---|---|---|
| Air Force | 20,600 | 32,800 | 39,300 | 48,500 | 48,700 |
| Navy | 8,200 | 12,500 | 20,900 | 26,900 | 27,500 |
| Marine Corps | 38,200 | 47,800 | 58,600 | 69,000 | 69,400 |
| Army | 116,800 | 143,000 | 158,200 | 239,100 | 279,500 |
| Total | 184,300 | 236,100 | 277,000 | 383,500 | 425,100 |

### U.S. Military Strength in Thailand

|  | Dec 65* | Mar 66* | Jun 66 | Dec 66 | Jun 67 |
|---|---|---|---|---|---|
| All services | 13,900 | 19,100 | + | + | + |

### U.S. Off-Shore Navy

|  | Dec 65* | Mar 66* | Jun 66 | Dec 66 | Jun 67 |
|---|---|---|---|---|---|
| Navy | 35,800 | 39,100 | 37,300 | 41,400 | 41,400 |

### U.S. and VNAF Attack Aircraft

|  | Dec 65* | Mar 66* | Jun 66 | Dec 66 | Jun 67 |
|---|---|---|---|---|---|
| Air Force | 367 | 450 | 547 | 644 | 644 |
| Marine Corps | 118 | 121 | 125 | 167 | 159 |
| Navy | 183 | 204 | 190 | 204 | 192 |
| Total | 668 | 775 | 862 | 1,015 | 995 |
| VNAF | 132 | 150 | 150 | 150 | 150 |

### U.S. Non-Attack Aircraft

|  | Dec 65* | Mar 66* | Jun 66 | Dec 66 | Jun 67 |
|---|---|---|---|---|---|
| Air Force | 306 | 350 | 457 | 677 | 712 |
| Navy | 18 | 26 | 29 | 25 | 25 |
| Marine Corps | 16 | 16 | 19 | 22 | 24 |
| Army | 369 | 402 | 411 | 466 | 532 |
| Total | 709 | 794 | 916 | 1,190 | 1,293 |

---

\* Data through Mar 66 is actual strength. Inaccuracies in manpower addition due to rounding of figures.
+ Not yet approved by OSD.

|  | Helicopters | | | | |
| --- | --- | --- | --- | --- | --- |
|  | Dec 65 | Mar 66 | Jun 66 | Dec 66 | Jun 67 |
| Air Force | 45 | 44 | 60 | 66 | 76 |
| Marine Corps | 193 | 214 | 238 | 250 | 280 |
| Navy | - | - | - | - | - |
| Army | 1,245 | 1,264 | 1,398 | 1,668 | 1,890 |
| Total | 1,483 | 1,522 | 1,696 | 1,884 | 2,246 |

|  | Maneuver Battalions | | | | |
| --- | --- | --- | --- | --- | --- |
|  | Dec 65 | Mar 66 | Jun 66 | Dec 66 | Jun 67 |
| U.S. Army/USMC | 35 1/3 | 45 2/3 | 52 2/3 | 70 | 79 |
| Other Allied | 10 | 10 | 14 | 23 | 23 |
| Vietnamese | 133 | 141 | 147 | 162 | 162 |
| Total | 178 1/3 | 196 2/3 | 213 2/3 | 255 | 264 |

McNamara's decisions restored 30 USAF attack aircraft originally scheduled for deployment to Southeast Asia by December 1966 but deleted by him on 26 March. However, he reduced by 72 (from 716 recommended by the JCS to 644) the number of attack aircraft scheduled for deployment by December 1966. By this date the USAF would have in place at least 31 jet attack squadrons.

### Requirements for Thailand and Other PACOM Areas

Throughout April the Air Staff, in conjunction with the other services and PACOM, reviewed again its personnel and unit requirements by the end of the year for areas other than South Vietnam as requested by McNamara. Believing that earlier estimates were excessive, the Defense Secretary provided criteria for determining force goals for Thailand, the Philippines, Taiwan, Japan, and the Ryukyu Islands. He also asked why units should be deployed to these countries rather than retained on call in Guam, Hawaii, and the United States. Service replies were to be prepared in cooperation with OSD's Southeast Asia Programs Division.[13]

On 29 April the JCS advised McNamara that a total of 46,937 additional U.S. personnel were needed in Thailand and the other PACOM areas, 14,813 of them Air Force. The service breakdown was given as follows:

|  | USAF | Navy | Marine | Army | Total |
|---|---|---|---|---|---|
| Thailand | 14,049 | - | - | 12,430 | 26,479 |
| Japan | 352 | - | 1,445 | 4,960 | 6,757 |
| Ryukus | 45 | 1,287 | 8,122 | 3,261 | 2,715 |
| Taiwan | 244 | - | - | - | 244 |
| Philippines | 123 | 619 | - | - | 742 |
| Total | 14,813 | 1,906 | 9,567 | 20,651 | 46,937 |

These figures included 567 (198 Air Force, 369 Army) advisory and counterinsurgency personnel to support the Thai government, and 9,567 Marines for the PACOM reserve and other deployments in Japan and the Ryukus.

In their "rationale," the Joint Chiefs explained that these estimates had been refined by Sharp and his commanders and were based on the concept submitted on 1 March.* This concept called for operational and logistic support of military activities in South Vietnam, North Vietnam, and Laos from Thailand and other Pacific bases, the introduction of major combat units into these countries if necessary, and an adequate reserve and logistic base to deter or defeat the Chinese Communists in Southeast Asia or elsewhere. They asked for early approval of the planning figures.[14] McNamara, however, made no immediate manpower decisions for areas outside of South Vietnam.

### Alignment of Air Munitions With Combat Sortie Needs

During April the Defense Secretary and the services also sought ways to ease a growing air ammunition shortage that threatened to limit the number of combat sorties. Deputy Defense Secretary Vance, while in Saigon at the beginning of the month, was informed that only 73 percent of the required bomb assets and only 33 percent of required CBU-2-type munitions were available.

---
* See p 19.

During an OSD-led conference in Honolulu, also in April, Westmoreland reported that insufficient munitions had caused cancellation or non-scheduling of 233 USAF sorties on 7 April and 134 sorties on the 8th.* He attributed the problem to late ship arrivals, delivery of some incomplete rounds of ammunition, and civil disturbances in Da Nang,+ an off-loading point. The conferees agreed to adopt an air sortie and air munition schedule for the last nine months of 1966, under which PACAF was allocated 141,966 strike sorties (out of a total of 278,216) and 251,015 tons of ammunition.

In the same nine-month period about 4,950 B-52 sorties would consume 90,000 tons of ammunition. USAF tactical aircraft would carry 2.4 tons per sortie in North Vietnam and 1.65 tons per sortie in South Vietnam.[15]

Reports of air munition shortages led Headquarters USAF on 19 April to activate a USAF logistic center in the Pentagon. Manned by transportation, production, programming, supply, logistic planning, and military assistance program (MAP) representatives, the center was responsible for monitoring and expediting shipment of air munitions to the war zone. The JCS and OSD used the center's reports to manage the overall munitions program. To bolster its Southeast Asia stocks, Headquarters USAF also asked and PACOM agreed to reallocate 30,000 more tons for Air Force use.[16]

Meanwhile, Sharp sent the results of the air munition conference to the JCS which, in turn, revised its monthly air sortie and air munition plan.

---

* Current and projected ammunition shortages affected USAF planning and operations in several ways. A temporary policy adopted in December 1965 requiring Seventh Air Force aircraft to land with their unexpended ordnance was extended; short ammunition loads were restricted to operations in South Vietnam and ammunition for training, exercises, and demonstrations were cut back if such use did not contribute directly or indirectly to the war effort in Southeast Asia.
+ See p 38.

Sent to McNamara on 10 May, it asked for quick approval to give Sharp a "base line" for firming up combat air sortie planning for the remainder of 1966. There was a cutback of about 8,000 PACAF sorties requiring ordnance, leaving 133,339 sorties for the April-December period. B-52 sorties were reduced from 4,950 to 4,350.

The JCS plan, as adjusted, was based on an overall service-weighted aircraft load of 1.66 tons per sortie using preferred ordnance. Each service was assigned specific tonnages above or below this average depending on operational areas and aircraft characteristics.[17] In computing the sortie-ammunition rates General McConnell, with JCS backing, had urged adoption of a policy of optimum air munition loads for all sorties flown to insure the most effective use of aircraft. Sharp ruled, however, that PACAF should use lighter munition loads if necessary to meet the planned sortie rate.[18]

On 24 May, after some further adjustments, McNamara approved the PACOM-JCS combat sortie program for South and North Vietnam and Laos for the last seven months of 1966. The monthly totals would rise from 28,055 sorties in June (USAF, Navy, Marines, and VNAF) to 33,337 sorties in December. McNamara said he still saw no need for the five USAF squadrons deferred on 10 March but he indicated he would reexamine requirements after more experience had been acquired with the sortie rate. He also opposed higher munition expenditures simply because aircraft could carry larger loads, thereby supporting Sharp's view.[19]

In late May and June OSD directed the Air Force and other services to expedite their munition deliveries to Southeast Asia in accordance with Sharp's request. Also, pending further JCS study, McNamara established a maximum tactical munition expenditure rate of 60,000 tons per month. He believed that this was all that could be used effectively.[20]

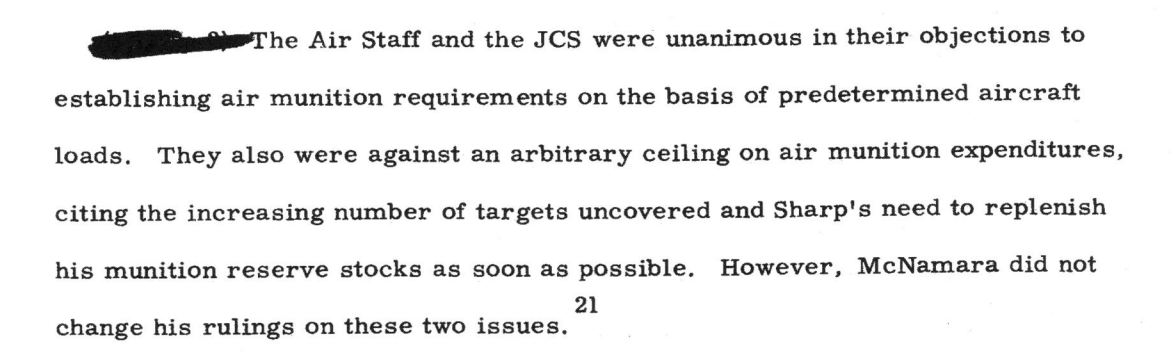

The Air Staff and the JCS were unanimous in their objections to establishing air munition requirements on the basis of predetermined aircraft loads. They also were against an arbitrary ceiling on air munition expenditures, citing the increasing number of targets uncovered and Sharp's need to replenish his munition reserve stocks as soon as possible. However, McNamara did not change his rulings on these two issues.[21]

## Lagging Air Base Construction

By the spring of 1966 further slippages in air base construction threatened to impede USAF's 31-jet tactical fighter squadron deployment program approved by OSD on 11 April.* Despite McConnell's efforts to hasten base expansion, it became clear that the lack of airfields in South Vietnam would delay deployment of two F-100 squadrons by two months and an F-4C squadron by three months. In May, Tuy Hoa, previously selected and dropped as a site, was again chosen, and OSD authorized the Air Force to initiate construction there using a civilian contractor. Its BOD was set for December 1966. Brown also pressed again for another air base after a site at Hue Phu Bai in the I Corps, recommended by the JCS on 27 April, was vetoed temporarily by the State Department because of civil strife in that region.[22]

In Thailand, new difficulties loomed. On 24 May McNamara informed Brown and other service secretaries that some of the construction projects there could not be justified. He asked they be halted until he, Deputy Secretary Vance, and other officials could determine if the work was necessary to support the currently approved military plan for Southeast Asia.[23]

## The War's Impact on Tactical Forces

The full impact of the Phase II deployment plan on USAF's tactical manpower, training, air munition, air base, aircraft, and other programs was

---
* See p 29.

reviewed in May by General McConnell and Gen. G. P. Disosway, Commander of TAC, before the Senate Preparedness Investigating Subcommittee. McConnell confirmed that the war had created an imbalance in the tactical force structure. He said that without a call-up of the Air National Guard, TAC could not continue to support large-scale augmentation and at the same time provide adequate forces for possible requests from NATO or for Cuba-type contingencies. He cited three main factors contributing to this situation: the drain on TAC resources to support Vietnam operations, the diversion of TAC combat units to train replacements, and aircraft attrition.

General Disosway reviewed these matters in more detail. He said that, although TAC thus far had filled all combat levies, his command would possess only four deployable combat squadrons by 30 July. He predicted that TAC manpower problems would be most critical from May through November 1966. Thereafter experienced personnel returning from Southeast Asia would become available to help correct deficiencies.[24]

The war's impact on USAF's tactical resources became more apparent at the end of June. In the preceding months TAC had sent five squadrons to Southeast Asia and three squadrons to USAFE on PCS assignment. Eighteen fighter squadrons were being used for training aircrew replacements and nine others were unequipped because of aircraft attrition in Southeast Asia.[25]

## OSD's 2 July Deployment Guidelines

On 2 July McNamara sent the Air Force and the other services revised guidelines for additional military deployments to Southeast Asia. Called Program 3,* it contained all proposed revisions and adjustments made since the issuance of the 11 April program. The Defense Secretary directed its use as the

---
* Dated 1 July 1966.

basis for further manpower and logistic planning and financial budgeting until he or Deputy Secretary Vance approved changes to it. He explained, subsequently, that Program 3 would give him a "handle" on and control of the U.S. buildup in Southeast Asia which he had not had thus far.[26]

Program 3 called for a rise in U.S. strength in South Vietnam to 431,000 by June 1967. The Air Force would have 634 attack-capable aircraft in the theater (out of a total of 982) by that date. U.S. and VNAF air ordnance expenditure would mount to 72,000 tons annually. The projected USAF attack aircraft strength for June 1967 was only 10 aircraft less than the 644 McNamara had approved in his earlier program guidance. Program 3 also listed past and projected USAF, Navy, and Marine Corps aircraft losses and loss rates.

On 15 July, at the request of President Johnson, McNamara submitted a brief report on the prospects for continued accelerated deployments to Southeast Asia for the remainder of 1966. He said there would be about 395,000 U.S. personnel in South Vietnam by year's end rather than 374,000 estimated in March. The Defense Secretary also indicated that more helicopters and maneuver battalions had been sent than previously thought possible. Although not officially reported to the President, only a few USAF aircraft--eight more F-104's and three more RB-66's--had been sent somewhat earlier than expected. The Air Staff observed that insufficient space at air bases was the principal reason USAF units had not been sent more expeditiously.[27]

## IV. NEW ESTIMATES OF U.S. 1966-1967 DEPLOYMENT NEEDS

By mid-1966, as a result of accelerated Phase II deployments, American air and ground forces in Southeast Asia had greatly increased. During the preceding six months, U.S. manpower in South Vietnam rose from 184,314 to 273,401 with USAF strength increasing from 20,620 to 37,772. In Thailand American strength rose from 14,609 to 24,470 with the USAF portion up from 9,117 to 17,789. (The war's impact also led to an overall USAF increase of 44,202 active duty personnel, bringing its total military manpower to 886,350). In the same period USAF tactical fighter, reconnaissance, special air warfare, and other aircraft nearly doubled in the two countries, rising from 731 to 1,438. Of the increased number of combat sorties (116,672) flown by the three services in South and North Vietnam and Laos in the first half of the year, USAF aircraft flew slightly over half. The percentages were: USAF, 51.6; Navy, 31.0; and Marine Corps, 17.4.[1]

(U) Despite the buildup, the war's progress was slow and at times the military situation regressed. The principal reason was a diminished South Vietnamese military and civil effort as Premier Ky's government struggled with public disorders in Hue and other Buddhist strongholds, precipitated by the dismissal on 10 March of Lt. Gen. Nyugen Chanh Thi, the I Corps commander. From mid-April to mid-May, the high point of the disorders, the level of military operations in the South was reduced by one-half. There were other difficulties. A spiraling inflation hurt the Vietnamese economy and was not rectified until June when there was a drastic devaluation of the local currency. A high desertion rate continued to plague the armed forces. Meanwhile, North Vietnam had stepped up its support of the Viet Cong.[2]

## Admiral Sharp's Revised 1966 and 1967 Requirements

The increasing Communist challenge prompted Admiral Sharp to prepare higher estimates of U.S. and allied military needs. There were submitted to OSD and the JCS on 18 June and reviewed at a Honolulu conference for McNamara on 8 July. The additional requirements, Sharp explained, were "created entirely" by North Vietnam's greater aid to the Viet Cong. An estimated 28,000 men had infiltrated into the south in the first five months of 1966 and the annual rate could reach 6,900 per month compared with 4,500 per month at the beginning of the year. The enemy was fielding more maneuver battalions than before, increasing the size of and improving the concealment of stockpiles in South and North Vietnam, strengthening his support organizations, and directing and controlling effectively ground forces up to division size.

Although the American air program had hurt the North Vietnamese, contributed to declining morale, and forced them to assign about 500,000 personnel to repair activities, Sharp felt the air and ground war would have to be intensified. He observed that earlier service recommendations to strike major ports of entry, POL targets, and logistic lines leading from China had not yet been authorized. Thus more air strikes were needed to reduce North Vietnam's support of Communist forces in the South. Intelligence placed Communist supply needs in South Vietnam at 240 to 255 tons per day. This would rise to 270 to 315 tons by December 1966, and to 350 tons at the end of 1967.

Sharp proposed including Laos in the stepped-up air effort with the aim of increasing the disruption and harassment of Communist supply lines. Additional reconnaissance should seek to uncover about 30 new targets each month, and he asked for additional USAF drones to supplement reconnaissance since they demanded less resources and their loss was not as serious as that of piloted vehicles.

For his 1966 adjusted requirements, Sharp recommended the deployment of 27,986 air, ground, and naval personnel in addition to the number already planned. About 14,870 would be Air Force and include the 5 tactical fighter squadrons that had been deferred, 8 C-123's for air-ground illumination (AGIL), 8 C-123's for defoliation, 8 AC-47's, 4 C-130's for airborne command centers (for a total of 7), 12 ARDF RC-47's (for a total of 47), and 3 CV-2 and 1 CV-2/7 squadrons (to be transferred from the Army to the Air Force in January 1967).* From the Army he desired three more air cavalry squadrons and other aviation units, and an augmentation of existing combat and engineer squadrons. The Navy increase would consist principally of one attack carrier (the sixth for the Seventh Fleet), four destroyers, and one guided missile destroyer.

For calendar year 1967 Sharp proposed the additional deployment of 121,000 personnel, of which 8,300 would be Air Force and include 5 tactical squadrons, 11 RF-4C's, 16 O-1's, 15 AC-47's, and 1 heavy and 2 medium repair squadrons. The Army would provide 11 more maneuver and other artillery and engineer battalions, more infantry and light tank companies, and air base defense units. The Navy would contribute one heavy cruiser, eight destroyers, supporting ships and personnel. The Marine Corps would add three helicopter companies and certain other air and ground units.

Sharp also envisaged a possible need for a corps contingency force in late 1967 or 1968 totaling 136,852 personnel (11,471 Air Force, 1,380 Navy, and 124,001 Army). USAF units would consist of eight tactical fighter, one tactical reconnaissance, and two troop carrier squadrons. The corps would improve the allied strength relative to the Communists and could significantly accelerate operations. For 1967 there would also be a need for more air- and sealift to support a Mekong Delta mobile afloat force (MDMAF), two more river

---

* Under the terms of an Air Force-Army agreement signed on 6 April 1966, the Army gave up its fixed-wing transports to the Air Force and the Air Force relinquished all claim to helicopters and follow-on rotary aircraft designed for intratheater movement, fire support, supply, and resupply. OSD approved the agreement on 13 April.

assault groups, and two more Army brigades--and possibly a third.

Excluding some forces only tentatively considered, Sharp thus proposed sufficient deployments to assure 524,800 U.S. and allied personnel (50,000 Air Force) in South Vietnam and 147,800 U.S. personnel (20,700 Air Force) in Thailand and other PACOM areas by the end of 1966. In 1967 he would dispatch 121,000 more U.S. and allied personnel (18,300 Air Force) to Vietnam and other PACOM areas. Adding to these forces a 136,800-man contingency corps, he visualized a grand total of 930,500 U.S. and allied personnel (90,300 Air Force) engaged in direct and indirect support of the war effort. U.S. and allied (but excluding Vietnamese) maneuver battalions would increase from 67 in July 1966 to 123 in December 1967. To support all ground units, including Vietnamese, and fulfill other air requirements combat air sorties would rise as follows:

|  | Jul 66 | Dec 66 | Jul 67 | Dec 67 |
|---|---|---|---|---|
| South Vietnam | 19,090 | 20,850 | 23,950 | 23,950 |
| North Vietnam and Laos* | 12,407 | 12,920 | 14,520 | 16,200 |
| Total | 31,497 | 33,770 | 38,470 | 40,150 |

To achieve these rates, Air Force, Navy, and Marine attack aircraft would fly about 7,000 more combat sorties per month at the end of 1967 than had been contemplated thus far.

## McNamara's Response

At the conclusion of the PACOM presentation at the Honolulu meeting, the Defense Secretary responded that it would be difficult to send all of the requested military forces into South Vietnam because of their possible inflationary impact, or into Thailand because the United States had not yet made a decision "to go it alone"

---

* Included 3,000 non-attack sorties.

there. The corps contingency force proposal needed a thorough review and he asked that it be considered separately. He promised to approve all deployments to sustain combat air sorties that could be used profitably, but he felt that air power was approaching a plateau in effectiveness where additional sortie capability would bring only marginal results.

USAF-Navy air operations against North Vietnam and Laos, McNamara said that his primary concern was unit destruction effectiveness. He thought that the amount of destruction per sortie was low and that there were probably sufficient sorties available. He said that it was President Johnson's wish that first priority should be given to complete "strangulation" of the North's POL system,* and that Sharp must not feel that there were sortie limitations to do this. He complimented the Air Force and Navy for their 29 June POL strike, calling it a "superb professional job," although he was highly incensed over the security leaks that preceded the mission. For more attacks on the POL targets it was essential to determine the North's land and sea distribution system, categorize the targets, and then render them ineffective.

Another important aspect of the "strangulation" campaign, he pointed out, was the need for increased interdiction of railroad lines, particularly bridges in the Northeast and Northwest leading to China. He was advised that PACAF had been assigned the rail lines in those areas beginning with Rolling Thunder 51,+ and had been directed to keep the lines out of operation for the

---

* In late May and early June, at the urging of Westmoreland, Sharp, Ambassador Henry C. Lodge, and the JCS, the administration approved USAF-Navy attacks on the previously exempt POL storage facilities of North Vietnam. These strikes, beginning 21 June, culminated in a USAF assault on 29 June that destroyed or damaged 95 percent of the facilities in Hanoi and a Navy attack on 29 and 30 June against similar targets near Haiphong. There also were follow-up strikes.
+ Rolling Thunder 51 began on 9 July 1966 and provided for armed reconnaissance for all of North Vietnam except a 30-mile radius around Hanoi, a 10-mile radius around Haiphong, and a 25- to 30-mile buffer zone bordering China. These "sanctuaries" were imposed in 1965.

maximum periods of time. The Defense Secretary believed that the interdiction program should be examined at a higher level (other than subordinate commands) and enjoined the Air Force to take the initiative in planning the application of air power. He suggested that the Air Staff evaluate in depth data received from PACAF.

On air ammunition, McNamara directed the services to adopt the production schedule in Program 3 that called for a levelling-off at 91,500 tons per month. He accepted Sharp's plan for an optimum expenditure of 2.05 tons per sortie with additional needs, if any, to come from world-wide stocks or production. He agreed with Sharp's proposal to increase the B-52 sortie rate to 600 per month in November 1966.

In discussing aircraft attrition, McNamara observed that USAF loss rates were lower and Navy's higher than planned. He said he was working with the services on reducing attrition and suggested that Sharp assist by adjusting USAF and Navy strike areas in North Vietnam.*

He was especially critical of the construction program. He thought that initial costs were satisfactory but that the large and expensive Air Force and other service follow-on proposals for expanding the South Vietnam bases at Da Nang, Chu Lai, Phan Rang, Qui Nhon, Cam Ranh Bay, Bien Hoa, and Tan Son Nhut were out of the question. He said that he and Secretary of State Dean Rusk were surprised to learn of the magnitude of the U.S. investment in Thailand and that

---

\* For the first six months of 1966 the total attack aircraft combat losses in Southeast Asia were as follows (average loss rates per 1,000 sorties in parenthesis): USAF, 78 (.129); Navy, 53 (.139); and Marine Corps, 15 (.073). There were, of course, many other losses due to other causes. As a result of a USAF briefing on aircraft attrition on 6 June, McNamara asked for more detailed analyses of the problem and on 19 July Secretary Brown, in conjunction with Navy studies, submitted an initial report. Others followed based on studies by the Operations Review Group within the Air Staff. To lessen aircraft attrition the JCS on 6 October recommended striking more North Vietnamese targets rather than shift USAF and Navy strike areas.

it could have occurred without their knowledge. In an "extremely blunt" review of this issue, he said that the United States was "going wild" on construction in that country, and warned that only costs directly related to the war would be approved. He indicated that Nam Phang AB, Thailand, would not become a main operating base and that other base construction would be pared down. However, he appeared to favor the plan for enlarging Sattahip AB, Thailand, and accepted the argument that by deploying 25 KC-135 tankers to Sattahip to support the B-52's, POL handling costs could be reduced. But the funds would have to come from the existing U.S. construction program for Thailand. He wanted the JCS to take a "hard look" at the overall construction program.

McNamara appealed to the conferees to keep expenditures within reasonable limits and solicited their understanding of this problem. Despite inflation, the administration wished to avoid imposing controls on the U.S. economy and on critical materials. Economic controls would further alienate public support for the war within Congress where some of the leadership was especially critical. He warned again that the United States would not commit itself to aiding Thailand's counterinsurgency efforts without the participation of at least one other major nation. He specifically noted that Great Britain had taken a stand against such participation.

The Defense Secretary emphasized that the administration was extremely concerned about border violations and said there would be no relaxation of present restrictions. He promised, however, to relax as necessary the sanctuaries around Hanoi and Haiphong, presently consisting of a 30-mile and a 10-mile radius, respectively, for each city.[3]

At the conclusion of the Honolulu conference, the senior USAF representative, Gen. Hunter Harris, Commander of PACAF, advised Headquarters USAF that he doubted that McNamara would approve the deployment of the five deferred USAF squadrons or the recommended sixth Navy aircraft carrier. Nevertheless, he thought that the Defense Secretary was pleased with air operations and would support all reasonable additional air requests. "I get the impression," Harris said, "that air will have better opportunities to have a decisive impact on /the/ future outcome of /the/ war in Vietnam."[4]

## Air Force Study of Sharp's Additional Requirements

Following the Honolulu conference, the Air Staff began a major review of the effects of Sharp's latest proposals on the USAF world-wide posture. To facilitate its analyses, the Air Staff on 15 July established an operational review group, an outgrowth of a smaller ad hoc study group set up in February.* The group gave special attention to aircraft attrition and other combat problems. Also, on 16 July the Air Staff organized a project entitled "Combat Strangler" to analyze specifically the application of air power as requested by McNamara at the Honolulu meeting.[5]

The Air Staff took the position that Sharp's latest proposals did not constitute a logical buildup of previously approved forces but rather were "additive." To determine if more U.S. military aid was needed, McConnell in early August proposed that the JCS endorse Sharp's 1966 adjusted and 1967 force requirements as valid for capability planning purposes only. Official JCS approval of further deployments should be contingent on the results of a continuous evaluation of the progress of the war--a recommendation made previously by the USAF Chief of Staff without success. But the other service chiefs did not agree with this suggestion. They did consent to hold a capabilities conference and to ask Sharp for more justification of some units.[6]

On 5 August the JCS sent McNamara its preliminary assessment of the impact of Sharp's additional force requests. It validated most of them except

---
* See p 16.

for the corps contingency force, which it said would be considered separately in accordance with the wishes of the Defense Secretary, and certain Air Force, Army, and Navy units that needed more study and justification. The Joint Chiefs said they planned to review PACOM and CIA estimates of Communist resupply strength in 1967 (there were some areas of disagreement), and some parts of Program 3 which did not include previously JCS-approved units and included others not approved. They also wished to review attack sortie estimates and the force calculations on which they were based. Service ability to meet the higher requirements would be examined at a capabilities conference scheduled for October in Honolulu. They said they would send the Defense Secretary a recommended deployment program by early November.

Taking cognizance of the recent air strikes the President had authorized against North Vietnam's POL storage areas, the Joint Chiefs recommended similar attacks against other targets. They warned that unless this were done, the deployment of ground units in addition to those advocated by Sharp might be needed.[7]

Meanwhile, Sharp amended his sortie requirements to provide for 800 B-52 sorties per month in 1967. This was requested by Westmoreland on 12 August who termed the B-52 operations "one of the major innovations of the war." He also desired to base the aircraft closer to South Vietnam to reduce their "reaction" time.[8]

To accomplish a more thorough analysis of USAF capabilities to support the war, Gen. Hewitt T. Wheless, Assistant Vice Chief of Staff, on 17 August sent new planning assumptions to Air Staff offices. He asked for further evaluation of Sharp's requests less certain manpower adjustments already agreed to by the USAF Directorate of Manpower and Organization. They were to consider all USAF resources in PACOM, rates of 1.1 and 0.8 sorties-per-aircraft-per-day for South Vietnam and Thai-based aircraft, support for the existing NATO commitment (which was provided by 18 tactical fighter squadrons and elements of three additional squadrons totaling 486 aircraft), and Congressional approval of a fiscal year 1967 supplementary military budget. The Directorate of Aerospace Programs was made responsible for the major analysis and the Directorate of Plans was to prepare the report for the Joint Staff. Observing that USAF forces had been taxed to the limit by the Southeast Asia war, Wheless enjoined the Air Staff to fullest cooperation in analyzing all problems.[9]

This work was completed by the Air Staff on 2 September. A major finding was that the Air Force could provide only 7 of the 10 additional tactical fighter squadrons desired by Sharp and then only by stretching out the deployments. Five could be deployed by November 1967 and two more in the first half of 1968. This information along with other service "inputs" was relayed to PACOM.[10]

In separate actions the Air Force and the other services also prepared answers to questions raised in "deployment issue" papers received from McNamara's staff. These were "line-by-line" analyses of Sharp's additional 1966 and 1967 requests. In forwarding these to the JCS in early August, the Defense Secretary said that while it was U.S. policy to send General Westmoreland all of the necessary weapons and supplies, excessive deployments could weaken U.S. ability to win the war by undermining South Vietnam's economic structure. From the Air Force he desired more justification for 14,979 personnel to man 10 USAF tactical fighter squadrons and three engineer squadrons for heavy repair and base operating support and to augment communication and computer activities. He asked whether gunfire from four more Navy destroyers might not substitute for about 1,300 sorties per month against North Vietnam. This would insure considerable savings as the annual cost to support three USAF squadrons was $300 million against an annual cost of only $25 million for four destroyers.*[11]

their reply of 24 September, the Joint Chiefs generally reaffirmed the need for the forces questioned in the deployment papers. But they agreed to reduce from 6,130 to 1,834 the number of personnel needed for USAF base operating support. They advised that the Air Force wished to review further the requirement for one tactical reconnaissance squadron (RD-4C) for South Vietnam and eight CV-2/7 aircraft for Thailand. They reaffirmed their views of 5 August which supported Sharp's concept or "war plan" of 18 June but noted that the proposed forces would be re-examined at the capabilities conference planned for October in Honolulu. They supported Sharp's combat sortie goals, asserting that "if the recommended strategy and concept for the air campaign against North Vietnam continues to be limited by political and materiel restraints, our efforts may not produce the desired results and could be costly."[12]

Not fully satisfied with this response to his initial deployment issue papers, McNamara on 6 October sent the service chiefs 28 more, including a request for more justification of some unit deployments. The papers questioned the need for 61,408 of a total of 92,122 U.S. personnel desired by the services for the remainder of 1966 and for 1967. From the Air Force McNamara wanted additional information on 20,127 of 22,436 personnel requested for fighter, airlift, and engineer units in South Vietnam and base support and communication personnel in Thailand.

---
* See p 60.

The Defense Secretary focused special attention on the proposal that 10 additional USAF squadrons and a sixth Navy carrier be deployed in order to generate 6,894 more combat sorties per month. He said that OSD's analysis of combat air requirements showed that no additional sorties were needed in South Vietnam because 3,340 sorties were available as a result of the decision to reduce air support to Vietnamese ground forces from 7,840 to 4,500 sorties per month.* Also, that four destroyers using gunfire could substitute for 1,300 sorties in striking North Vietnam targets in areas 7 to 10 miles from the sea.+ Further, OSD's analysis indicated that additional armed reconnaissance sorties thus far had not affected the enemy's overall night resupply and infiltrating system, nor would they force the enemy to enlarge the 300,000-man work force now engaged in bridge, road, and other repair activities. Intelligence reports and aerial reconnaissance clearly showed that the interdiction program effectively harassed and delayed truck movement of materiel into South Vietnam but had no effect on troop infiltration moving along trails almost completely invisible from the air. In addition to these points, it was evident that the cost to the enemy to replace trucks and cargo that could be destroyed by more combat sorties was negligible compared with the estimated U.S. loss of 230 aircraft costing $1.1 billion over the next two years as a consequence of stepping up air attacks. What was needed, said McNamara, were improved tactics and equipment--

---

\* See p 60.
+ Use of naval gunfire on land targets in North Vietnam had been long under study. On 13 May the JCS recommended its use between the 17th and 20th parallel. But on 15 October and 18 November OSD approved only naval gunfire against North Vietnam's waterborne military and logistic targets between the 17th and 18th parallel. On 29 November, backed by Westmoreland and Sharp, the JCS recommended the use of both artillery and naval gunfire on targets immediately north of the demilitarized zone. At year end a decision on hitting land targets with naval guns was still held in abeyance at the highest government level.

and better strategy such as the barrier concept* rather than more air forces.

By not deploying additional USAF squadrons, cancelling the requirement for about 5,500 base support personnel (excluding those at Tuy Hoa AB), and rejecting a proposed air base at Hue Phu Bai+ in the I Corps, McNamara anticipated substantial dollar savings. The estimated cost of constructing the latter was $50 million and it was in an area that had political problems. The savings would also remove a potential inflationary impact on South Vietnam's economy.

other issues McNamara believed that the Air Force had overstated its manpower needs. Considered excessive were 1,341 personnel to augment CV-2 squadrons in South Vietnam after 1 January 1967, many of the 1,225 personnel desired for intratheater airlift, and personnel for four of six additional communication units. He thought that a 1,870-man U.S. engineering force supported by 1,000 local nationals in Thailand would suffice and permit the deletion of one medium repair squadron planned for Korat AB. He questioned 610 spaces earmarked for a counterinsurgency dispersal base in Thailand to relieve alleged overcrowding at Nakom Phanom AB.[13]

### The Impact on the Air Force's World-Wide Posture

Almost simultaneous with the receipt of McNamara's 28 deployment issue papers in early October, the Joint Chiefs sent him a preliminary assessment of the impact of Sharp's 1966 adjusted and 1967 force requirements

---

* After many months of study McNamara on 15 September directed that planning and preliminary work begin on establishing an air and ground barrier system near the demilitarized zone from the South China sea across the northern boundary of South Vietnam, and across Laos to the Mekong river boundary with Thailand. Lt. Gen. Alfred D. Starbird, Director of the Defense Communications Agency, was appointed to head the project, designated Joint Task Force 728.
+ See p 35.

on the U.S. world-wide military posture.  Citing U.S. strategic objectives as outlined in a JCS paper of 24 September 1965[*] and McNamara's guidance concerning additional deployments,[+] they concluded that approval of Sharp's requests would affect adversely the services, the unified and specified commands (except PACOM), and entail undue risk.  The major impact on the Air Force was depicted as follows:

1. Inability to deploy rapidly by June 1967 U.S.-based tactical fighter forces.  With one exception, all fighter and reconnaissance squadrons by that date would be committed entirely to training.

2. A reduction in USAFE tactical fighter strength from 21 (486 aircraft) to 13 squadrons (288 aircraft) by the end of September 1967.  There would also be a temporary withdrawal of all aircraft with electronic countermeasures (ECM) and electronic intelligence (ELINT) capability.  The fighter force could be built up to within 72 aircraft of its previous strength of 486 aircraft by the end of fiscal year 1968.

3. A deficit in the first quarter of fiscal year 1968 of the Strike Command (STRICOM)'s capability to meet NATO and other contingencies, the shortage being 22 tactical fighter squadrons assuming current rates of aircraft attrition and production.

4. A drastic pilot shortage incompatible with the U.S. commitment to NATO, with USAFE barely meeting its nuclear strike plan needs.  Any

---

[*] The strategic objectives were: with allied forces, maintain forward deployment to deter Communist aggression; possess a capability to support NATO/European obligations with ready, deployable forces through the first months of M/D (mobilization day) plus 30 in the event of imminence of hostilities; possess a capability to conduct other contingency operations where force commitments were minor but crucial; support military operations in Southeast Asia; and maintain an adequate training and rotation base.

[+] No call-up of reserve forces, extensions of terms of service, or changes in rotation policies; the services should rely on world-wide military resources.

increase in Southeast Asia deployment would aggravate this situation.

5. Air base shortages that could be alleviated only by a new base in South Vietnam, completion of Nam Phong AB, Thailand as a main operating base, and additional construction on other bases in the two countries.[14]

The effect on USAFE already was severe. In July General McConnell had directed the withdrawal of 110 USAFE tactical fighter aircrews to assure a 100-percent manning in Southeast Asia (or a 1.5:1 ratio). This action reduced USAFE's manning to a 1:1 ratio or about 80 percent and had had an adverse impact on the nuclear strike plan. Various actions were subsequently taken to minimize withdrawals from USAFE, and that command took extraordinary measures to preserve its capability.[15]

The problems of USAFE and other deficiencies were spelled out in accompanying documents. Only prompt approval of all requested forces and additional training and rotation requirements could reconstitute the Air Force's strategic reserve. The Air Staff considered the availability of trained personnel, especially aircrews, to be the overriding problem.* The full effect of Sharp's 1966 and 1967 requirements was tabulated as follows:[16]

---

* On 5 August McConnell ordered the establishment of a special Air Staff study group to examine manning and personnel replacements in Southeast Asia. As a result of the group's work he instructed General Harris, the PACAF commander, to assign qualified staff officers to "cockpits" regardless of inconvenience, and to take other measures to overcome the shortage. In early October he limited, beginning January 1967, pilot-rated officers in Headquarters USAF to three-year tours of duty.

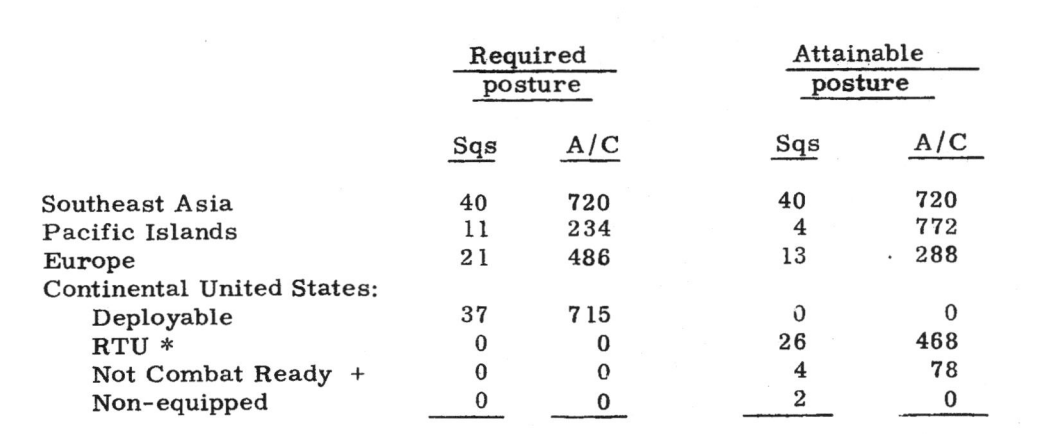

|  | Required posture | | Attainable posture | |
|---|---|---|---|---|
|  | Sqs | A/C | Sqs | A/C |
| Southeast Asia | 40 | 720 | 40 | 720 |
| Pacific Islands | 11 | 234 | 4 | 772 |
| Europe | 21 | 486 | 13 | 288 |
| Continental United States: | | | | |
|    Deployable | 37 | 715 | 0 | 0 |
|    RTU * | 0 | 0 | 26 | 468 |
|    Not Combat Ready + | 0 | 0 | 4 | 78 |
|    Non-equipped | 0 | 0 | 2 | 0 |
| Total | 109 | 2,155 | 89 | 1,626 |

The Army and Navy also described how the proposed deployments affected their military posture.

---

\* In the event of international tension, the replacement units could become deployable in two to six weeks but this would end all training.
\+ In training or in the process of being equipped.

## V. YEAR-END DECISIONS

From 5 to 15 October service representatives again convened in Honolulu to hold the long-planned capabilities conference on Sharp's augmented 1966 and 1967 force requirements. McNamara's deployment issue papers had suggested that he would not endorse them fully. In addition, the Defense Secretary was preparing to leave for Saigon to review the war's progress, the pacification program, and the economic impact of higher deployments on South Vietnam's economy.[1]

### The Honolulu Conference of October

In preparation for the October session, USAF and other service submissions were sent to PACOM through the Joint Staff. There they were incorporated into three volumes that contained the latest intelligence estimates, a modified strategic concept, an air program, lists of combat forces and logistic units, and deployment schedules.[2]

Intelligence briefings indicated that in July and August Viet Cong and North Vietnamese combat, guerrilla, support, and political cadre strength, despite losses, had again risen in the South, from about 271,070 to 281,192 personnel. During the previous 90 days the enemy had expanded his infiltration routes in Laos and Cambodia and an entire North Vietnamese division had moved across the demilitarized zone (DMZ) into the South. Supply capability from the North to the South was up from 308 to 460 tons per day. Aircraft strength was placed at 46 MIG-15/17's, 15 MIG-21's, and 6 IL-28's.

Discussing future Communist strategy, PACOM intelligence briefers thought Hanoi had three basic options: fight with larger forces up to division size, increase multi-battalion operations in widely scattered areas, or revert to guerrilla-type warfare. They believed that the first possibility was the most likely. Headquarters MACV was concerned especially about the buildup in the DMZ and predicted that the North Vietnamese would attempt to seize key objectives in the I Corps. To thwart this move Westmoreland would require more troops. However, Admiral Sharp, General Harris, and the Navy and Marine Corps component commanders disagreed, believing that MACV was over-emphasizing the threat of division-size forces. In their view the heavy air attacks on lines of communication were severely hurting the enemy's capability for such operations. Furthermore, any troop massings could be more easily destroyed by tactical and B-52 aircraft. In support of this view, Admiral Sharp cited recent evidence of Communist shortages of food, medicine, ammunition, and other supplies. The service representatives also did not support MACV requests for more infantry units to defend air bases, since other Army officials had stated this could be provided best by normal patrol and offensive operations.

Sharp recommended continuance of the basic strategy previously adopted: exerting more air and naval pressure on the North, destroying Communist forces and their infrastructure in the South, and assisting the Saigon government in "nation building." He thought that about 50 percent of the total 1967 military effort in South Vietnam would be used for direct support of the "revolutionary development" or pacification program. Logistic studies showed that current and recommended combat forces could be supported. As for the overall air program, Sharp reaffirmed his requirements of 18 June, but believed the target base in North Vietnam should be broadened.

The conferees reviewed recent Air Staff and other service studies that indicated the deployments would have to be stretched out to June 1968. Of 10 additional USAF tactical fighter squadrons still needed--and endorsed by the JCS--only seven could be provided. The proposed schedule called for the deployment of four squadrons to South Vietnam in September and November 1967 and January and May 1968, and two squadrons to Thailand in April and one in September 1967. USAF and Marine Corps aircraft would average 1.1 sorties-per-aircraft-per-day except USAF A-1's which would average 1.2. USAF Thai-based aircraft, including A-26's, would average .8.

proposal to reequip the combat arm of the VNAF was discussed. The VNAF's A-1's (six squadrons) would be transferred to USAF's special air warfare force from September 1966 through March 1968, and the fighter force reconstituted beginning with non-jet A-26's in October 1966 and jet AT-37's and F-5's from April 1967 through March 1968.* Its combat rate would be .8 sorties-per-aircraft-per-day.

The conferees were advised that the proposed sixth aircraft carrier for the Seventh Fleet would not be added.

The principal additional ground forces would consist of 12 U.S. Army maneuver battalions deployed between August and November 1967, and one Australian Army battalion in April 1967. The six U.S. Marine Corps and Korean Army battalions previously requested would not be available. Sharp recognized that all military requirements could not be met in accordance with the time schedule of 18 June, since to do so would affect too adversely the U.S. world-wide military posture. Nevertheless he believed that the situation in South Vietnam dictated fulfilling his needs as effectively as possible while minimizing the impact of deployments on U.S. military readiness elsewhere.[3]

Sharp proposed that the number of tactical fighter squadrons in South Vietnam be increased from 37 in January 1967 (22 USAF, 15 USMC) to 40

---

* On 13 July OSD had approved Secretary Brown's 18 June recommendation that the VNAF's six A-1 squadrons be converted to two F-5 and four AT-37 squadrons. Subsequent OSD guidance reduced this to one F-5 and three AT-37 squadrons. USAF's "Skoshi Tiger" F-5 aircraft would transfer to the VNAF and be replaced by an F-4C unit.

by June 1968 (26 USAF, 10 USMC, 4 VNAF)[*]. For Thailand he proposed an increase of USAF squadrons from 11 to 14. Combat sorties in all areas should rise from 37,150 in January 1967 to 39,550 by December 1967, and maintain this rate through June 1968. This sortie goal was only slightly less than the 40,150 per month recommended at Honolulu on 8 July.

In South Vietnam, combat sorties were still calculated on the basis of 150 per month for U.S., Korean, and Australian Army battalions, and 200 per month for U.S. and Korean Marine battalions, however, requirements for Vietnamese Army battalions, based on recent experience, were reduced from 7,800 to 4,500 sorties per month.[+] Land-based tactical reconnaissance needs would be met by an increase from 8.5 squadrons in January 1967 to 9.5 squadrons in December 1967, all but one of them Air Force.

The conferees observed that the tactical fighter and reconnaissance squadrons would be stationed on eight air bases in South Vietnam and five in Thailand. The need for Nam Phong AB, Thailand, as a main operating base, rather than as a "bare base" as McNamara had ordered on 8 July, was reaffirmed. Three other USAF squadrons (of the 10 desired) were still earmarked for deployment to the proposed but still not approved new base at Hue Phu Bai in the I Corps.[4]

While these matters were being reviewed at the capabilities conference, Westmoreland completed for the JCS a review of his deployment needs and an assessment of McNamara's 28 deployment issue papers of 6 October. He also quickly prepared for McNamara, who visited Saigon from 9 to 14 October, three "balanced force" deployment "packages" wherein the impact of U.S. military forces on the South Vietnamese economy would not exceed 46-, 44-, and 42-billion piasters. McNamara advised U.S. officials that, in

---
[*] Except for two USAF A-1 squadrons, by June 1968 all squadrons would be jets.
[+] See p 60.

the absence of a crisis, they were not to exceed a 46-billion piaster ceiling, and that Westmoreland should plan on a maximum U.S. strength in South Vietnam of no more than 470,000 troops. If possible, McNamara desired to reduce the piaster expenditure ceiling to 42 billion. This level was strongly backed by Ambassador Lodge to avoid accelerated inflation which would compound the Saigon government's still "tenuous and precarious" position.

In his report to McNamara, Westmoreland, after weighing both his military and revolutionary development (pacification) requirements, said that there were sufficient combat air sorties for South Vietnam. He agreed with earlier PACOM recommendations calling for more sorties in North Vietnam and Laos to hit "multiple, small, fleeting, and perishable" targets, and validated a rate of 16,200 combat sorties per month for both countries. He called attention to the 3,890 combat sortie deficit that loomed for this purpose. The shortage was attributed principally to the "stretch-out" in deployment of seven USAF squadrons and the unavailability of the sixth aircraft carrier for the Seventh Fleet. Sharp endorsed Westmoreland's report.[5]

A second report, prepared at McNamara's request, revised downward PACOM's needs as outlined initially on 18 June and generally confirmed at the capabilities conference in Honolulu. In sending it to the JCS on 23 October, Sharp observed that the formula for establishing the piaster deployment packages had not been proved by experience. He noted that only troop deployments and construction work were subject to complete U.S. management control. Other factors, such as those affecting the South Vietnamese economy, were not as amenable to U.S. direction.[6]

### The Air Force-JCS Position on Sharp's 1966-1967 Needs

The Air Staff generally supported Sharp's and Westmoreland's latest evaluations and conclusions on force requirements, especially on air power.

However, new uncertainty arose whether the Air Force would be able to provide all seven additional USAF tactical fighter squadrons. Following the Air Staff analysis of 2 September that indicated their availability, higher aircraft and aircrew losses since July 1966, Sharp's projected greater losses, stepped-up tactical fighter rotations, and OSD changes in fighter aircraft procurement, had altered considerably the basis of the USAF estimate.

Accordingly, the Air Staff called for another study. Completed on 21 October, a few days after the close of the capabilities conference, it showed that only four rather than seven squadrons would be available, two in April and two in September 1967. As the shortage would not occur for about a year, it was possible that it might be overcome if in the interim there were changes in the aircraft attrition rate, sortie allocations, and aircraft procurement and training policies.[7]

On 4 November the Joint Chiefs sent their findings and recommendations to McNamara. They contained with some adjustments Sharp's and Westmoreland's manpower requirements, air program, intelligence estimates, and a concept for deploying the military units. The concept was a modification of previous ones and included military actions not yet authorized such as mining the ports of and imposing a "naval quarantine," against North Vietnam, and conducting certain "spoiling" attacks and special operations against Communist forces in Laos and Cambodia. Excluded from the JCS recommendations was Sharp's proposed corps contingency force and OSD's infiltration barrier project.

Endorsing Sharp's sortie allocations, the Joint Chiefs recommended deploying five more USAF tactical fighter squadrons in 1967 and two more in 1968 (of the 10 previously desired). Neither the three USAF squadrons nor a sixth carrier for the Seventh Fleet were considered. They noted that certain Army ground and helicopter units that were desired were not available.[8]

▓▓▓▓▓▓▓ Almost simultaneously the JCS, after receiving the views of Westmoreland and Sharp, replied to questions raised in McNamara's 28 deployment issue papers of 6 October. Concerning those relating to the Air Force and Navy, the JCS stated:

1. Admiral Sharp's Southeast Asia air campaign would require 39,550 combat sorties per month (by the end of 1967 and through June 1968), of which 23,350 would be needed to support 118 maneuver battalions (including 4,500 for the Vietnamese Army). A sortie deficit in North Vietnam of about 4,000 could be met best by using air assets in South Vietnam, Thailand, and carrier aircraft.

2. It did not follow that sorties excess to Vietnamese Army requirements could be allocated to deficit areas. The reduction in sorties for the Vietnamese (from 7,800 to 4,500 per month) resulted from increased emphasis on security and pacification tasks and on U.S.-Vietnamese combined operations. Meanwhile, deployment of more U.S. and allied forces would generate 3,300 additional sorties per month.

3. It was incorrect to assume that naval gunfire could substitute for strike aircraft and that there could be a cost-effective "trade-off" between them. Sharp's recommendation envisioned naval gunfire as supplementary to rather than a substitute for tactical air. Naval gunfire could not satisfy quick-reaction requirements nor would its use in lieu of aircraft constitute employment of the most effective weapon.

4. Concerning interdiction effectiveness, the cost to the enemy was not measured solely by the loss of trucks but in lost capability to pursue his objectives in South Vietnam. From the standpoint of cost-effectiveness, the best way to maximize enemy and minimize U.S. costs was to strike trucks before they left concentration centers--areas that could not be hit because of political restraints.

5. The importance of the interdiction campaign could be seen by the high priority North Vietnam was giving to constructing another land route parallel to Route 1A in route packages 2 and 3. Interdiction also discouraged "outside" contribution of assets that might be destroyed before they could be used.

6. The current type of air campaign with its restraints maximized the exposure of aircraft to well-defended targets of limited value.

7. Improved interdiction strategy was needed but this did not necessarily include use of an infiltration barrier. Although the barrier concept had not been subjected to cost analysis, its effectiveness was open to serious question and the financial outlay could well exceed (OSD's) anticipated losses of $1.1 billion worth of aircraft over the next two years.

8. An effective air campaign against North Vietnam should include closing ports and attacks on the air defense system, airfields, and other high value targets for which authorization had thus far been denied.

On other Air Force matters the service chiefs replied that if only two of five more USAF squadrons desired for South Vietnam were approved, the proposed base at Hue Phu Bai in the I Corps would not be essential. They also advised that disapproval of a medium repair squadron at Korat AB (with 400 men) would mean either reconstituting Prime Beef* TDY teams or renegotiating with U.S. contractors presently in Thailand who were already overworked, and that the 610 spaces proposed for a counterinsurgency dispersal base in Thailand could be deleted. In addition, they reconfirmed, adjusted, or deleted lesser requirements questioned by McNamara relating to USAF airlift, communication, medical evacuation, and other support personnel.

With respect to inflation in South Vietnam, the JCS agreed that the problem was important but should not be "over-riding in determining force levels

---

* Prime base engineering emergency force.

above those recommended." Westmoreland's three force level packages did not cost out precisely at 42-, 44-, and 46-billion piasters because operational requirements to insure balanced forces prevented precision.

In view of the foregoing, the JCS recommended an increase in U.S. and allied (free world) forces directly and indirectly supporting the war from 591,662 at the end of 1966 to 782,056 at the end of 1968. The breakdown was as follows:

### South Vietnam

|  | End 1966 | End 1967 | End 1968 |
|---|---|---|---|
| USAF | 54,322 | 60,635 | 62,606 |
| Navy | 24,292 | 34,712 | 35,204 |
| USMC | 65,188 | 71,039 | 71,039 |
| Army | 238,954 | 330,782 | 355,439 |
| Total | 382,756 | 497,168 | 524,288 |
| FWMAF | 51,059 | 51,059 | 51,059 |
| Grand Total | 433,815 | 548,227 | 575,347 |

### Thailand and other PACOM Areas

|  | End 1966 | End 1967 | End 1968 |
|---|---|---|---|
| USAF | 83,020 | 90,048 | 90,048 |
| Navy | 24,771 | 33,087 | 33,367 |
| USMC | 23,806 | 46,625 | 48,928 |
| Army | 26,250 | 31,380 | 34,366 |
| Total | 157,847 | 201,140 | 206,709 |

USAF strength in this period would increase from 137,342 personnel and 33 tactical fighter squadrons to 152,654 personnel and 40 tactical fighter squadrons. The Joint Chiefs considered the overall buildup less then desired but thought it would suffice to support Sharp's concept of operations. Higher force levels could not be met without the administration revising certain of its policies, such as permitting a call-up of reserves or extending terms of service.[9]

## McNamara's Deployment Decisions

After weighing these recommendations, McNamara on 11 November informed the JCS that the proposed forces for South Vietnam were too large. He stressed the need for a stable economy in that country and the danger of runaway inflation. To avoid disrupting price stability achieved in the summer of 1966, McNamara said that actions already were being taken to reduce military and construction piaster spending. Even the spending ceiling of 42 billion desired by Ambassador Lodge might leave an inflationary gap of 10 billion piasters but it probably would hold the price rise down to 10 to 25 percent in 1967 compared with 75 to 90 percent in fiscal year 1966.

The Defense Secretary said that inflation hit heaviest at Vietnamese soldiers and civil servants on whom success largely depended. Army desertions and civilian departures from the civil service could cancel the effect of more U.S.-allied deployments, raise the spectre of civil strife, seriously hamper military and pacification efforts, and possibly lead to the collapse of the Saigon government. JCS recommendations would cost more than 46 billion piasters in 1967 and would be self-defeating. McNamara's deployment objectives for South Vietnam, compared with JCS recommendations, were as follows:

### Comparison of JCS and OSD Deployment Plans

|  | Jun 67 JCS* | Jun 67 OSD | Dec 67 JCS* | Dec 67 OSD | Jun 68 JCS* | Jun 68 OSD |
|---|---|---|---|---|---|---|
| USAF | 60,600 | 55,300 | 63,300 | 55,400 | 65,300 | 55,400 |
| Navy | 32,100 | 27,600 | 35,300 | 29,400 | 35,800 | 29,400 |
| USMC | 70,600 | 70,600 | 70,600 | 70,600 | 70,600 | 70,600 |
| Army | 292,600 | 286,000 | 334,800 | 307,900 | 350,500 | 313,900 |
| Total | 455,900 | 439,500 | 504,000 | 463,300 | 522,200 | 469,300 |

The Defense Secretary's figures called for 16,400 fewer U.S. troops at the end of June 1967, 40,700 fewer at the end of December 1967, and 52,900 fewer at the end of June 1968.

* Adjusted figures after the JCS submission of 4 November.

Details of the above approved deployments were incorporated in a Program 4 sent by McNamara on 18 November to the JCS, the services, and other OSD offices. Compared with Program 3 issued on 2 July 1966,* the major changes consisted of extending the deployment program through fiscal year 1968, limiting air munition expenditures to 64,000 tons per month (with 1,500 tons per month for training beginning 1967), and increasing the B-52 sortie rate to 800 per month beginning February 1967. Tactical aircraft sorties and losses were updated by OSD to reflect the best estimates, and the piaster expenditure plan was adjusted to coincide with the approved piaster budget through June 1967. Program 4 represented the latest manpower and logistic planning guidelines for fiscal budgetary purposes. McNamara invited the services to "change the mix" of forces, and solicited their views on ways to accelerate deployments to insure the maximum combat capability early in 1967. Highlights of Program 4 were as follows:[11]

### U.S. and VNAF Attack Sorties

|  | Oct 66+ | Dec 66‡ | Jun 67 | Dec 67 | Jun 68 |
|---|---|---|---|---|---|
| South Vietnam | 11,746 | 14,567 | 14,348 | 13,110 | 12,861 |
| North Vietnam | 8,656 | 9,566 | 10,746 | 9,877 | 11,793 |
| Laos | 2,310 | 4,422 | 3,186 | 4,348 | 2,815 |
| Total | 22,712 | 28,555 | 28,280 | 27,335 | 27,469 |
| B-52 | 410 | 650 | 800 | 800 | 800 |

---
*See pp 36-37.
+ Actual sorties.
‡ Current plan, Dec 66 through Jun 68.

### U.S. and VNAF Fighter and Attack Aircraft

|  | Oct 66* | Dec 66+ | Jun 67 | Dec 67 | Jun 68 |
|---|---|---|---|---|---|
| USAF | 598 | 664 | 646 | 646 | 646 |
| USMC | 160 | 167 | 159 | 159 | 159 |
| Navy | 200 | 215 | 184 | 193 | 178 |
| Total | 958 | 1,043 | 989 | 998 | 983 |
| VNAF | 109 | 119 | 108 | 72 | 90 |
| Total | 1,067 | 1,166 | 1,097 | 1,070 | 1,073 |

### U.S. Non-Attack Aircraft

|  | Oct 66 | Dec 66 | Jun 67 | Dec 67 | Jun 68 |
|---|---|---|---|---|---|
| USAF | 480 | 578 | 738 | 742 | 742 |
| Navy | 28 | 32 | 24 | 26 | 26 |
| USMC | 45 | 30 | 46 | 46 | 46 |
| Army | 454 | 504 | 486 | 562 | 562 |
| Total | 1,007 | 1,144 | 1,284 | 1,376 | 1,376 |

### Helicopters

|  | Oct 66 | Dec 66 | Jun 67 | Dec 67 | Jun 68 |
|---|---|---|---|---|---|
| USAF | 65 | 79 | 74 | 86 | 86 |
| Navy | - | - | - | - | - |
| USMC | 293 | 254 | 280 | 280 | 280 |
| Army | 1,652 | 1,601 | 2,098 | 2,642 | 2,801 |
| Total | 2,010 | 1,934 | 2,452 | 3,008 | 3,167 |

### USAF Fighter and Attack Aircraft

|  | Oct 66 | Dec 66 | Jun 67 | Dec 67 | Jun 68 |
|---|---|---|---|---|---|
| A-1 | 37 | 50 | 50 | 50 | 50 |
| A-26 | 8 | 8 | 8 | 8 | 8 |
| B-57 | 21 | 24 | 24 | 24 | 24 |
| F-100 | 156 | 198 | 198 | 198 | 198 |
| F-102 | 21 | 30 | 30 | 30 | 30 |
| F-104 | 16 | 18 | 18 | - | - |
| F-105 | 133 | 126 | 126 | 90 | 90 |
| F-4 | 180 | 180 | 180 | 234 | 234 |
| F-5 | 15 | 18 | - | - | - |
| T-28 | 11 | 12 | 12 | 12 | 12 |
| Total | 598 | 664 | 646 | 646 | 646 |

\* Actual aircraft and helicopter strength.
+ Current plan, Dec 66 through Jun 68.
‡ The VNAF began receiving a few A-26's in Oct 66 and was scheduled to receive F-5's and AT-37's from Apr 67 through Mar 68. Its A-1's would be returned to the Air Force.

USAF Non-Attack Aircraft

|  |  |  |  |  |  |
|---|---|---|---|---|---|
| RB-57 | 3 | 4 | 4 | 4 | 4 |
| EB-66 | 20 | 28 | 32 | 32 | 32 |
| RF-4 | 52 | 60 | 60 | 60 | 60 |
| RF-101 | 33 | 32 | 32 | 32 | 32 |
| AC/C-47/54 | 37 | 42 | 42 | 42 | 42 |
| RC-47 | 17 | 45 | 47 | 47 | 47 |
| EC-121 | 4 | 3 | 3 | 3 | 3 |
| C-123 | 76 | 84 | 84 | 84 | 84 |
| C-130* | - | - | 4 | 4 | 4 |
| KC-135 | 31 | 37 | 40 | 40 | 40 |
| CV-2 (C-7A) | - | - | 96 | 96 | 96 |
| O-1/O-2 | 182 | 195 | 246 | 250 | 250 |
| U-10 | 15 | 32 | 32 | 32 | 32 |
| HU-16 | 2 | 5 | 5 | 5 | 5 |
| HC-130H | 8 | 11 | 11 | 11 | 11 |
| Total | 480 | 578 | 738 | 742 | 742 |

USAF Helicopters

|  |  |  |  |  |  |
|---|---|---|---|---|---|
| UH-1 | 14 | 15 | - | - | - |
| HH-43 | 29 | 34 | 34 | 40 | 40 |
| HH-53 | - | - | 4 | 4 | 4 |
| HH-3 | 10 | 16 | 22 | 28 | 28 |
| CH-3 | 12 | 14 | 14 | 14 | 14 |
| Total | 65 | 79 | 74 | 86 | 86 |

Thus both air and ground forces desired by Sharp and the JCS were reduced. Combat sorties were dropped from a proposed peak of 39,350 per month to between 28,000 and 29,000 per month. There also were reductions in the number of attack, reconnaissance, transport, and special air warfare aircraft, in helicopters, and in maneuver, engineer, and artillery battalions. Only B-52 sorties would increase.

McNamara had approved a 650-sortie per month rate for the B-52's while visiting Saigon in October and the JCS ordered its implementation on the 26th.

---

* Assigned to Southeast Asia beginning Jan 67. Twelve C-130 squadrons were based in Japan, Okinawa, and the Philippines to support operations in South Vietnam and Thailand.

But SAC delayed augmenting the bomber and supporting tanker force (for a total of 50 B-52's on Guam and 40 KC-135's on Okinawa) to sustain this rate until President Johnson completed his tour of Asia.* The new rate did not go into effect until about 20 November. Meanwhile, on 11 November McNamara further approved a rate of 800 sorties per month beginning 1 February 1967. This would require a total of 70 B-52's.

The need for more bombers to sustain higher sortie rates, now strongly backed by General Westmoreland[+], focused additional attention on long-considered but controversial plans to station them nearer the war theater. Basing in South Vietnam appeared unwise for reasons of cost, logistics, and vulnerability, and the State Department interposed strong political objections to their operations from Okinawa or Taiwan. As a consequence, General McConnell and Secretary Brown urged OSD to place the bombers on Sattahip AB, (redesignated U-Tapao on 10 August) in Thailand, but this recommendation also posed difficulties. McNamara was concerned lest the Thai government exact "heavy gratuities" for permitting B-52's in Thailand and he desired additional intelligence assessments of Communist China's possible reaction to such a step. At year's end no firm decision had been taken.[12]

### Air Force-JCS Reaction to McNamara's Decisions

In a review of McNamara's force deletions, the Air Staff observed they included seven USAF tactical fighter squadrons, 136 other fixed-wing aircraft, mostly Air Force, and 265 Army helicopters. The 136-aircraft total contained the following principal USAF units: 3 CV-2 squadrons for South Vietnam, 2 C-130 squadrons for Thailand (previously deferred), 15 AC-47's for South Vietnam and

---

\* President Johnson visited Southeast Asia from 17 October to 2 November.
+ See p 46.

Thailand, 10 EB-66's for Thailand, 8 C-123's (AGIL) for South Vietnam, and 1 F-100 squadron. The last was scheduled to replace the F-5 squadron after its aircraft were transferred to the VNAF. Also eliminated were 12,005 USAF support personnel, including 8,159 for South Vietnam and 3,846 for Thailand and other PACOM areas.[13]

On 2 December the services informed McNamara of the impact the reduced forces in Program 4 would have on the war effort. McConnell's comments on the USAF program were as follows:

1. Elimination of the seven fighter squadrons would affect adversely the air effort, especially in the North and in Laos, stretch out the time needed to achieve air objectives in Southeast Asia, reduce the intensity of the war in an area where it would hurt the enemy most, and lower the Air Force's capability to respond to emergency or contingency situations.

2. The 10 EB-66's were needed to protect strike aircraft, and to provide timely and usable electronic reconnaissance for all forces.

3. The JCS had authorized the deployment of the 8 AC-47's and aircrews on 27 June and they were already at Clark AB. If they were not sent to South Vietnam, Westmoreland would be denied important aerial support for hamlet and base defense against Viet Cong mortar and other attacks. Further, the cost of repairing damaged aircraft and facilities or rebuilding friendly hamlets might well be greater than any savings accrued by not deploying the aircraft.

4. The deletion of 361 support personnel for the ARDF RC-47's would lower the capability of these unique aircraft and the effectiveness of their equipment.

5. The engineer repair squadron at Korat AB, Thailand, was needed for heavy work and for constructing facilities at reduced costs. Its deletion would adversely affect other engineering activities.

6. Medical support personnel and aircraft were badly needed to assure faster medical evacuation and to assume some duties formerly performed by Army personnel.

Not cited by McConnell were deletions that would reduce night interdiction and airlift capability and hamper the projected anti-infiltration barrier program. He also wished to send three C-7A squadrons to South Vietnam, as requested earlier by Westmoreland. The need for such units had been confirmed by Secretary Brown after a visit to Asia. He informed McNamara on 6 October that one of Sharp's biggest problems was airlift: intratheater, intertheater, and intercountry.[14]

(TS-Gp 4) In an overall assessment of McNamara's decisions, McConnell joined the other service chiefs in advising the Defense Secretary that his force ceilings would restrict U.S. combat capabilities in South Vietnam, particularly in the I Corps unless "serious" withdrawals were made from other corps. It would curtail projected opening of land lines in the II, III, and IV Corps important to both military operations and the revolutionary development (pacification) program, and diminish U.S. support in extending the Saigon government's control over the country. In sum, the reduced forces would affect the war's momentum and possibly result in a larger conflict at more cost and casualties.

Reaffirming their recommendations of 4 November, the JCS warned that while the restoration of economic stability in South Vietnam was important, it depended primarily on sufficient forces to defeat the enemy, to secure the country for political, social, and economic development, and to give impetus to pacification. They asked McNamara to exempt some forces that did not affect piaster expenditures. These consisted of certain USAF, Army, and Navy units operating outside of South Vietnam, and service personnel away on rest and recuperation.

4) As suggested by McNamara, the services made some adjustments in the "mix" of deployments. In South Vietnam the Air Force asked for about 300 more personnel for a TAC fighter wing headquarters at Phu Cat AB and a hospital at Cam Ranh Bay. Nearly an equal number of personnel would be deleted by changing the status of the 602d Air Commando Squadron from TDY to PCS. This unit was assigned to South Vietnam but stationed at Udorn AB, Thailand. The Navy requested trade-offs involving about 2,000 personnel and the Army about 12,700 personnel. In Thailand, the Army proposed changes involving about 400 personnel.[15]

4) On 9 December McNamara approved the adjustments except for certain Army requests that needed more justification. He thought that Program 4 likewise was adequate for other PACOM areas, stipulating that "any additional requests for deployments to out-of-country areas should be fully justified as to their relation to the conflict in Southeast Asia."[16]

McNamara's Program 4 decisions also required adjustments in air munition allocations. At the end of the year, Sharp submitted new Air Force and other service estimates in accordance with the Defense Secretary's guidelines. He stressed especially the need for more 1,000-, 2,000-, and 3,000-pound bombs, CBU/ADV munitions, and Shrike air-to-ground missiles. The Air Force and Navy secretaries earlier had urged renewed production of the 2,000- and 3,000-pound bombs, the first for use in Southeast Asia and the second for stockpiling. OSD subsequently approved production of 2,000-pound bombs but made no immediate decision on 3,000-pound bombs pending more study and testing.[17]

### The Year-End Situation

As 1966 ended U.S. military personnel in South Vietnam stood at 390,568 and in Thailand, 34,489. Within these totals were 52,889 and 26,892

# TOP SECRET

## PACAF AIRCRAFT DEPLOYMENT
### 26 Dec 66

**Tainan**
4/EC-121
5/F-100
TOTAL - 9

**Chiang Chuan Kang**
50/C-130
TOTAL - 50

**Naha**
28/F-102
53/C-130
5/HU-16
TOTAL - 86

**Kadena**
3/HH-43
49/F-105
1/C-130
37/KC-135
TOTAL - 90

**Kunsan**
7/F-100
TOTAL - 7

**Osan**
15/F-105
2/HH-43
TOTAL - 17

**Yokota**
21/F-105
1/RB-47
2/HH-43
4/EB-57
TOTAL - 28

**Misawa**
11/F-100
2/HH-43
TOTAL - 13

**Binh Thuy**
34/O-1
1/HH-43
5/AC-47
TOTAL - 40

**Nha Trang**
2/C-47      16/U-10
3/HC-47     15/C-123
1/HH-43     58/O-1
1/AC-47     8/RC-47
TOTAL - 104

**Itazuke**
2/KC-135
TOTAL - 2

**Tachikawa**
16/C-124
14/C-130
5/HC-130
TOTAL - 35

**Muang Ubon**
38/F-4
2/HH-43
TOTAL - 40

**Pleiku**
20/A-1
5/AC-47
2/HH-43
6/RC-47
TOTAL - 33

**Hickam**
6/HC-97
4/EC-135
2/HC-130
TOTAL - 12

**Takhli**
59/F-105
3/HH-43
9/KC-135
22/EB-66
TOTAL - 93

**Guam**
49/B-52
2/KC-135
4/HC-130
2/EB-47
TOTAL - 57

**Tuy Hoa**
60/F-100
1/HH-43
TOTAL - 61

**Clark**
27/C-130
28/F-102
26/B-57
4/HU-16
2/HH-43
14/F-100
1/RB-47
7/AC-47
2/KC-135
TOTAL - 111

**Don Muang**
4/F-102
TOTAL - 4

**Mactan**
24/C-130
TOTAL - 24

**U-Tapao**
22/KC-135
TOTAL - 22

**Korat**
76/F-105
2/HH-43
TOTAL - 78

**Udorn**
15/RF-101
18/A-1
4/HH-3
6/F-102
9/CH-3
18/F-104
4/HC-130
22/RF-4
2/HH-43
TOTAL - 98

**Nakhon Phanom**
3/HH-3
23/O-1
15/UH-1
7/A-26
11/T-28
15/U-6
6/UC-123
TOTAL - 80

**Tan Son Nhut**
1/C-47
14/RF-101
3/RB-57
4/EC-121
31/C-123
2/HH-43
40/RF-4
4/CH-3
11/RC-47
TOTAL - 110

**Bien Hoa**
70/F-100
62/O-1
2/HH-43
3/DC-130
15/F-5
5/AC-47
2/U-2
6/F-102
12/UC-123
TOTAL - 177

**Phan Rang**
2/HH-43
73/F-100
20/B-57
TOTAL - 95

**Cam Ranh Bay**
79/F-4
2/HH-43
TOTAL - 81

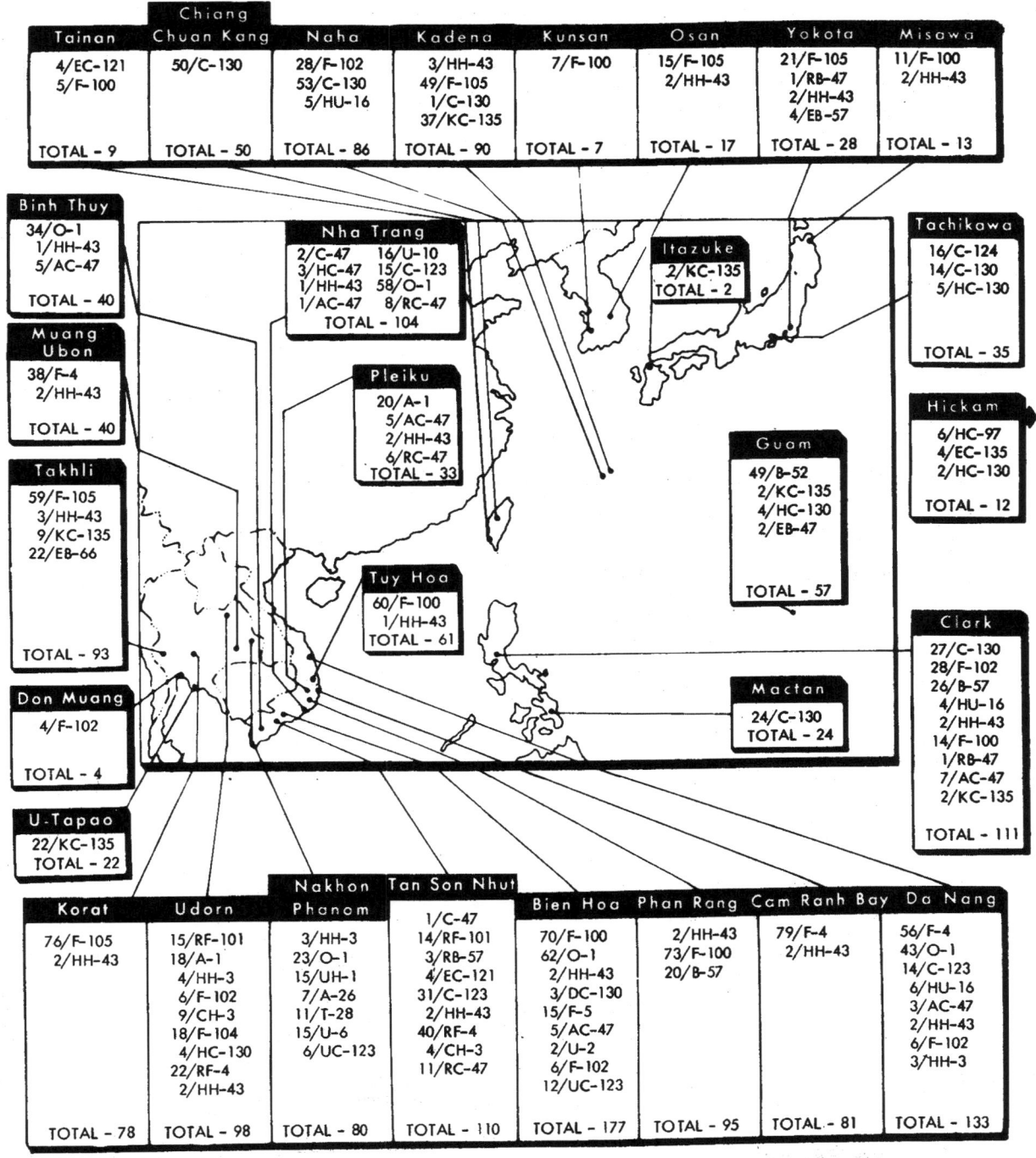

**Da Nang**
56/F-4
43/O-1
14/C-123
6/HU-16
3/AC-47
2/HH-43
6/F-102
3/HH-3
TOTAL - 133

Source: Status of Forces Report
(1-AF-V21), 26 Dec 66

# TOP SECRET

(This page is SECRET-NOFORN)

USAF personnel, respectively. The Air Force also had deployed to the two countries 822 and 412 aircraft, respectively, including 61 helicopters. The total consisted of 640 attack and 533 non-attack aircraft, excluding the helicopters.*[18] In JCS deliberations during the year on courses of action in and deployments to Southeast Asia, McConnell--while avoiding "splitting" JCS papers--had pressed for better use of available forces, especially air power, rather than a massive ground buildup. He also urged the JCS frequently to evaluate the war's progress to help determine the best use of forces, but this project moved very slowly. One Air Staff assessment at year's end disclosed no significant trend toward attaining U.S. military objectives in Southeast Asia. However, it pointed to certain accomplishments. U.S.-allied air and ground actions had prevented a Communist seizure of South Vietnam, caused a major drain on North Vietnam's manpower and resources, "spoiled" many enemy operations, and created psychological shock, especially with B-52 bombings of training areas and supply points. In the last three months of the year there were fewer large-scale Communist operations.

The prospect for 1967 was for heavier fighting in South Vietnam and more infiltration of men and supplies from the North. Although some members of the Air Staff in late 1966 believed that the Communists were possibly changing their tactics from large-scale to guerrilla-type actions, a study of USAF intelligence and reports from Sharp and Westmoreland did not fully support this conclusion. Communist regular, militia, and political cadres strength at the end of December was estimated at 280,575 personnel, about 15,500 more than at the beginning of the year despite losses in excess of 90,000 in the 12-month period.+ The Viet Cong and North Vietnamese still appeared capable of replacing their losses by local recruitment or

___
* Manpower figures are as of 31 Dec 66; aircraft figures as of 2 Jan 67. USAF aircraft in the two countries plus other attack and non-attack aircraft in other PACOM areas gave PACAF a total of 1,773 aircraft of all types to support U.S. objectives in Asia. See p

+ In comparison, South Vietnamese and U.S. losses in 1966 were about 9,500 and 5,000 killed, respectively.

## PACAF AIRCRAFT SUMMARY
### 2 JAN 67

| AIRCRAFT | SVN | THAILAND | ISLANDS | PACAF |
|---|---|---|---|---|
| A-1 | 22 | 15 | - | 37 |
| A-26 | - | 7 | - | 7 |
| AC-47 | 18 | - | 7 | 25 |
| B-52 | - | - | 50 | 50 |
| B-57 | 20 | - | 26 | 46 |
| C-47 | 4 | - | - | 4 |
| C/UC-123 | 71 | 6 | - | 77 |
| C-124 | - | - | 16 | 16 |
| C-130 | - | - | 165 | 165 |
| CH-3 | 4 | 9 | - | 13 |
| DC-130 | 3 | - | - | 3 |
| EB-57 | - | - | 4 | 4 |
| EB-66 | - | 22 | - | 22 |
| EC-121 | 4 | - | 4 | 8 |
| EC-135 | - | - | 4 | 4 |
| F-4C | 129 | 41 | - | 170 |
| F-5 | 15 | - | - | 15 |
| F-100 | 206 | - | 35 | 241 |
| F-102 | 12 | 10 | 56 | 78 |
| F-104 | - | 18 | - | 18 |
| F-105 | - | 134 | 85 | 219 |
| HC-47 | 3 | - | - | 3 |
| HC-97 | - | - | 5 | 5 |
| HC-130 | - | 4 | 11 | 15 |
| HH-3 | 3 | 7 | - | 10 |
| HH-43 | 15 | 9 | 11 | 35 |
| HU-16 | 6 | - | 9 | 15 |
| KC-135 | - | 32 | 47 | 79 |
| O-1 | 185 | 22 | - | 207 |
| RB-57 | 3 | - | - | 3 |
| RC-47 | 27 | - | - | 27 |
| E/RB47 | - | - | 4 | 4 |
| RF-4C | 40 | 22 | - | 62 |
| RF-101 | 15 | 15 | - | 30 |
| T-28 | - | 11 | - | 11 |
| UH-1F | - | 14 | - | 14 |
| U-2 | 2 | - | - | 2 |
| U-6 | - | 14 | - | 14 |
| U-10 | 15 | - | - | 15 |
| TOTAL | 822 | 412 | 539 | 1,773 |

Source: Status of Forces Report, 2 Jan 67

infiltration from the North. MACV thought infiltration averaged 5,240 per month for the year.

In view of the Communist buildup, it remained to be seen whether the air and ground deployment levels approved in November--well below those recommended by the JCS--and the strategy emphasizing ground operations in South Vietnam and severely restricted air operations in North Vietnam and Laos, would achieve U.S. objectives. Analyses of the war gave General McConnell and the Air Staff no reason to alter their long-held views that greater use of air power, especially against North Vietnam, was the only alternative to a long, costly war of attrition in Southeast Asia.[19]

NOTES

### Chapter I

1. Jacob Van Staaveren, USAF Plans and Operations in Southeast Asia, 1965, (TS), (hereinafter referred to as Van Staaveren), (AFCHO, 1966), pp 90 and 99; memo (S), G. Ball, Under Secy of State to SECDEF, 17 Jan 66, no subj: memo, Col J. K. Lambert, Dep Dir of Aerospace Programs, DCS/P&R to AFCHO, 15 May 66, subj: Draft AFCHO Hist Study (TS).

2. Van Staaveren, pp 8, 39, 90, 92; DAF order no 559N, 26 Mar 66 (U).

3. Testimony of SECDEF R.S. McNamara, 26 Jan 66, in House Hearings before Subcmte of the Cmte on Appn, 89th Cong, 2d Sess, Supplemental Defense Appropriations for 1966, pp 30-32; Van Staaveren, pp 30 and 37; background briefing by U.S. officials (U), 31 Jan 66, in SAFIO.

4. Senate Rprt of Sen. Mike Mansfield et al to Cmte on Foreign Relations, 6 Jan 66, subj: The Vietnam Conflict: The Substance and the Shadow (U), pp 11-12; Wash Post, 2 Jan 66; N.Y. Times, 6-9 Feb 66.

5. Memo (TS), CSAF to SAF, 6 Jan 66, subj: Reprogrammed Phase Force Rqmts for CY 1966; Van Staaveren, p 71.

6. Memo (TS), CSAF to SAF, 6 Jan 66; memo (TS), Maj Gen S.J. McKee, Asst DCS/P&O for JCS to CSAF, 4 Mar 66, subj: U.S.-GVN-FW Progress in SVN; CSAFM-Y-16-66 and CMCM-133-66 (TS), 5 Jan 66; Hist (TS), Dir/Plans, Jan-Jun 66, p 26.

7. CSAFM-Y-16-66 and CMCM-133-66 (TS), 5 Jan 66.

8. Memo (TS), SAF to SECDEF, 10 Jan 66, subj: Reprogrammed Rqmts for CY 1966; memo (TS), SAF to SECDEF, 17 Jan 66, subj: AF Capability to Meet CINCPAC's Rqmts.

9. Memo (TS), Col J.H. Germeraad, Asst Dep Dir/Plans for War Plans to CSAF, 25 Feb 66, subj: Deployments to SVN, w/atch (TS), Background Paper on SEA Strategy vs Deployments; Van Staaveren (TS), pp 67-69.

10. JCSM-16-66 (TS), 8 Jan 66; memo (TS), SECDEF to Chmn JCS, 19 Jan 66, subj: Air Ops Against NVN; N.Y. Times, 7-14 Jan 66; Balt Sun, 6 Jan 66.

11. Ltr (TS), Lt Gen J.T. Carroll, Dir DIA to SECDEF, 21 Jan 66, subj: An Appraisal of the Bombing of NVN; CSAFM-32-66 (TS), 12 Jan 66; JCSM-41-66 (TS), 18 Jan 66; CM-1134-66 (TS), 25 Jan 66.

12. Memo (TS), SECDEF to Chmn JCS, 22 Jan 66, subj: Air Ops Against NVN; JCSM-56-66 (TS), 25 Jan 66; CM-1134 (TS), 25 Jan 66.

13. Memo (TS), Maj Gen R. N. Smith, Dir/Plans to CSAF, 12 Feb 66, subj: Employment of Air Power in the War in VN; N.Y. Times, 1 Feb 66; Wash Post, 1 Feb 66; Background Paper (TS), Division of R/T Areas, Mar 66.

14. Memo (TS), Smith to CSAF, 12 Feb 66; CM-1147-66 (TS), 1 Feb 66; Hist (S), Dir/Ops, Jan-Jun 66, p 26; ltr (TS), CINCPAC to JCS, 18 Sep 66, subj: Eval of CY 66 and CY 67 Force Rqmts, w/atch (TS), Hq MACV Rprt, 5 Sep 66, subj: Eval of Capabilities of Friendly Forces to Accomplish Objectives and Tasks; study (TS), An Eval of the Effects of Air Campaign Against NVN and Laos, prep by Jt Staff, Nov 66.

### Chapter II

1. Ltr (TS), CINCPAC to JCS, 12 Feb 66, subj: CY 66 Capabilities Prog; ltr (TS), Maj Gen J.W. Vogt, DCS/P&O, Hq PACAF to Hq USAF, 12 Feb 66, subj: Phase IIA Eval, w/atch (TS) Rprt on Eval of Forces, undated; JCS 2343/769-1 (TS), 16 Feb 66; memo (TS), McKee to C/S USAF, 24 Mar 66, subj: Air Ops Against Aflds in NVN; memo, Col E.F. MacDonald, Asst Chief, Combined Plans Div, DCS/P&O to C/S USAF, 25 Feb 66, subj: Deployment Sched for SEA and other PACOM Areas; background briefing (U), 31 Jan 66; Hist (TS), Hq MACV, 1966, p 127; Van Staaveren (TS), p 43.

2. JCS 2343/772 (TS), 18 Feb 66; memo (TS), SOD to Pres, 24 Jan 66, subj: The Mil Outlook in SVN (TS).

3. Hist (S), Dir/Plans, Jan-Jun 66, pp 7-8; Hist (S), Dir/Ops, Jan-Jun 66, pp 5-6 and Jul-Dec 66, pp 10-14 (U); memo (U), Dep SECDEF to Secys Mil Depts et al, 19 Feb 66, subj: Estb of SEA Prog Div; memo (S), Lt Gen H.T. Wheless, Asst Vice CSAF, to Vice CSAF et al, 16 Feb 66, subj: Estb of a Study Effort to Review Current Tac Sortie Rqmt for SEA; memo (TS), MacDonald to CSAF, 25 Feb 66; SM-170-66 (TS), 21 Feb 66.

4. Memo (TS), MacDonald to CSAF, 25 Feb 66; SM-170-66 (TS), 21 Feb 66, JCS 2343/760-5, 24 Feb 66 (TS).

5. Memo (TS), MacDonald to CSAF, 25 Feb 66.

6. Hist (TS), Dir/Plans, Jan-Jun 66, pp 60-63; memo (S), Col F.L. Kaufman, Asst Dep Dir for War Plans, DCS/P&O to CSAF, 25 Feb 66, subj: Afld Const; memo (C), SAF to SECDEF, 8 Feb 66, subj: Feasibility of AF Const for AB and Related Const in VN.

7. Msg 99717 (TS), CSAF to PACAF, 12 Feb 66; memo (TS), SECDEF to Mil Depts et al, 17 Feb 66, subj: SEA Deployment Planning Assumptions; memo (S), SAF to SECDEF, 19 Feb 66, subj: Decision Rqmts Associated with SEA Deployment Planning Assumptions; Hist (S), Dir/Aerospace Progs, Jan-Jun 66, p 29.

8. JCSM-130-66 (TS), 1 Mar 66, w/atch (TS), Apps A and B; JCS 2343/760-9 (TS), 7 Mar 66; memo (TS), SECDEF to Secys of Mil Depts et al, 10 Mar 66, subj: Deployments to SEA.

9. Memo (TS), McKee to CSAF, 8 Mar 66, subj: Log Implications for CY 66 Deployments to SEA and World-Wide Mil Posture.

10. Memo (S), SAF to SECDEF, 3 Mar 66, subj: SEA Deployment Planning; memo (TS), McKee to CSAF, 31 Mar 66, subj: Deployment Prog for SEA and Other PACOM Areas.

11. Memo (TS), SECDEF to Secys of Mil Depts et al, 10 Mar 66, subj: Deployments to SEA.

### Chapter III

1. Memo (S), Dep SECDEF to Secys of Mil Depts, 21 Feb 66, subj: Special Pers Proc to Support SEA Rqmts; memo (S), Under SAF to Asst SECDEF (Manpower), 11 Mar 66, same subj, both in OSAF; Hist (S), Dir/Pers Planning, Jan-Jun 66, p 81.

2. Memo (S), Lt Gen G.W. Martin, IG Hq USAF, to SAF, 22 Mar 66, subj: Congestion in RVN, in OSAF; memo (S), McKee to CSAF, 31 Mar 66, subj: Deployment Prog for SEA and other PACOM Areas; memo (S), SAF to SECDEF, 19 Mar 66, subj: Afld Const; Hist (S), Dir/Plans, Jul-Dec 66, pp 275-76; CSAFM-E-31-66 (TS), 2 Mar 66.

3. Memo (S), SAF to SECDEF, 19 Mar 66.

4. Memo (TS), SAF to SECDEF, 21 Mar 66, subj: Deployments to SEA.

5. Memo (TS), McKee to CSAF, 11 Apr 66, subj: Tac A/C Rqmts; Hist (S), Dir/Aerospace Progs, Jan-Jun 66, p 71; memo (TS), SECDEF to Chmn JCS, 26 Mar 66, subj: Tac A/C Rqmts for SEA; JCS 2343/760-18 (TS), 31 Mar 66.

6. Memo (TS), McKee to CSAF, 4 Apr 66; JCSM-215-66 (TS), 2 Apr 66; JCS 2343/760-18 (TS), 31 Mar 66; memo (TS), McKee to CSAF, 11 Apr 66, subj: Tactical A/C Rqmts in SEA.

7. Memo (TS), SAF to SECDEF, 21 Mar 66, subj: Deployments to SEA; memo (S), J.T. McNaughton, Asst SECDEF (ISA) to Col B.R. Daughrety, Exec Asst to SAF, et al, 25 Mar 66, subj: Reduction in European Forces.

8. Memo (TS), SECDEF to SAF, 31 Mar 66, subj: Deployments to SEA.

9. Hist (U), Dir/Pers Planning, Jan-Jun 66, pp 81-83; Records (S), Dir/Plans.

10. JCSM-218-66 (TS), 4 Apr 66; JCSM-274-66 (TS), 28 Apr 66; memo (TS), SECDEF to Chmn JCS, 12 Mar 66, subj: JCSM-218-66.

11. Memo (TS), Col R.W. Lucia, Asst Dep Dir for War Plans to Asst for Jt and NSC Matters, DCS/P&O, 9 Apr 66, subj: Deployment of five TFS in CY 66 and CY 67; memo (TS), McKee to CSAF, 11 Apr 66; JCSM-233-66 (TS), 15 Apr 66; memo (TS), McKee to CSAF, 25 Apr 66, subj: Deployment Prog for SVN.

12. Memo (TS), SECDEF to Secys of Mil Depts et al, 11 Apr 66, subj: SEA Deployment Plan, w/atch, 10 Apr Plan; memo (S), SECDEF to Chmn JCS, 2 Apr 66, subj: Deployments to PACOM (Other than SVN).

13. Hist (TS), Dir/Plans, Jan-Jun 66, pp 30-31; memo (S), SECDEF to Chmn JCS, 2 Apr 66, subj: Deployment to PACOM (Other than to SVN).

14. Hist (TS), Dir/Plans, Jan-Jun 66, pp 30-31; JCSM-272-66 (TS), 29 Apr 66; memo (S), Sec Def to Chmn JCS, 2 Apr 66.

15. Memo (S), McKee to CSAF, 13 Apr 66, subj: Ammo Situation in SEA; Hist (S), Dir/Ops, Jan-Jun 66, pp 29-30; JCS 2343/760-69 (TS), 28 Jun 66; Hist (TS), Hq MACV, 1966, p 256.

16. Memo (S), Acting SAF to SECDEF, 10 May 66, subj: Mun Supp Capability, FY 67; Hist (S), Dir/Transp, Jan-Jun 66, pp 51-52.

17. Memo (S), McKee to CSAF, 6 May 66, subj: Air Munition Consumption and Distribution Plan in SEA; JCSM-417-66 (TS), 9 May 66.

18. CSAFM-V-22-66 (S), 4 May 66; memo (S), McKee to CSAF, 6 May 66; Hist (S), Dir/Plans, Jan-Jun 66, pp 58-59.

19. Memo (TS), SECDEF to Chmn JCS, 24 May 66, subj: Air Mun and Sortie Plan for SEA.

20. Memo (C), P.R. Ignatius, Asst SECDEF (I&L) to SAF et al, 27 May 66, subj: Air Mun SEA, in OSAF; memo (S), Maj Gen J.C. Sherrill, Special Asst for Strat Mobility, JCS to Ignatius, 21 Jun 66, subj: Exped Movement of Air Mun to RVN; memo (U), Ignatius to Secys of Mil Depts et al, 23 Jun 66.

21. JCS 2343/760-69 (TS), 28 Jun 66; JCSM-445-66 (TS), 2 Jul 66.

22. Hist (TS), Dir/Plans, Jan-Jun 66, pp 60-63; Hist (S), Dir/Aerospace Progs, Jan-Jun 66, pp 71-72; JCS 2343/818 (TS), 26 Apr 66; CSAFM-V-31-66 (S), 13 May 66; memo (S), SAF to SECDEF, 27 May 66, subj: Afld Rqmts for SEA; memo (S), Dep SECDEF to SAF, 27 May 66, same subj: memo (S), Smith to CSAF, 17 Jun 66, subj: Afld Const.

23. Memo (TS), SECDEF to SAF et al, 24 May 66, no subj.

24. Testimony (TS) of Gen J.P. McConnell, CSAF and Lt Gen G.P. Disosway, Comdr TAC, 9-10 May 66, before Senate Preparedness Investigating Subcmte of Cmte on Armed Services, 89th Cong, 2d Sess, pp 3-7 and 40-70.

25. Hist (S), Dir/Aerospace Progs, Jan-Jun 66, p 22.

26. Memo (TS), SECDEF to Secys of Mil Depts et al, 2 Jul 66, subj: SEA Deployment Plan; msg 100625 (TS), CINCPACAF to CSAF, 10 Jul 66.

27. Memo (TS), Pres to SECDEF, 28 Jun 66; memo (S), SECDEF to Pres, 15 Jul 66, no subj: memo (TS), Smith to CSAF, 5 Jul 66, subj: CINCPAC CY 1966 Deployments; Hist (TS), Dir/Plans, Jul-Dec 66, pp 361-63.

## Chapter IV

1. USAF Mgt Summary (S), 1 Jul 66, pp 8 and 26; DOD News Release 64-67, 25 Jun 67; Draft (U), DOD Annual Rprt for FY 66, p 62; JCS 2343/235-1 (TS), 6 Oct 66, Testimony of SAF on 30 May 66(U), in Senate Hearings before Subcmte of the Cmte on Appns and the Cmte on Armed Services, DOD Appropriations for FY 1967, pt I, p 866.

2. N.Y. Times, 11 Mar, 4 Apr, 19 Jun, and 5 Jul 66; Balt Sun, 12 Jun 66. background briefing by U.S. officials (McNamara et al) (U), 11 Jun 66, in SAFOI.

3. Hist (S), Dir/Ops, Jul-Dec 66, p 20; memo (TS), Smith to CSAF, 16 Jun 66, subj: NVN Air Strike Prog; msgs 100625 and 100630 (TS), CINCPACAF to CSAF, 10 Jul 66; memo (TS), Asst SECDEF (SA) to Secys of Mil Depts et al, 12 Jul 66, subj: CINCPAC Jul 8, 1966 Briefing, in OSAF; ltr (TS), CINCPAC to JCS, 4 Aug 66, subj: CINCPAC Briefing for SOD, 8 Jul 66; memo for record (S), by Maj W.F. McConnell, Jun 66, subj: A/C Attrition; memo (S), SAF to SECDEF, 19 Jul 66, subj: A/C Attrition in SEA; JCSM-698-66 (TS), 2 Nov 66; memo (S), SECDEF to Chmn JCS, 13 Jul 66, subj: Establishing Limits on DOD Piaster Spending in VN; JCS 2343/889 (TS), 25 Aug 66; N.Y. News, 24 June 66; N.Y. Times, 24, 28, 29, 30 Jun and 1 and 10 Jul 66; JCSM-645-66 (TS), 6 Oct 66; Hist (S), Dir/Aerospace Progs, Jan-Jun 66, pp 22-23.

4. Msg 100625 (TS), CINCPACAF to CSAF, 10 Jul 66.

5. Hist (S), Dir/Ops, Jul-Dec 66, pp 10 and 20-21; memo (TS), Smith to Dir/Ops, 28 Jun 66, subj: CINCPAC's CY 66 Adjusted Rqmts and CY 67 Rqmts; memo (TS), Brig Gen R.D. Rheinbold, Dep Dir of Plans for War Plans to Dep Dir of Plans for Policy, 7 Jul 66, same subj.

6. Hist (TS), Dir/Plans, Jan-Jun 66, pp 26-27; memo (TS), Maj Gen L.D. Clay, Jr., Dir/Plans to CSAF, 30 Jul 66, subj: CINCPAC CY Adjusted Force Rqmts and 1967 Force Rqmts; CSAFM-H-1-66 (TS), 1 Aug 66.

7. Hist (TS), Dir/Plans, Jul-Dec 66, pp 349-51; memo (TS), Lucia to Asst Dir for Plans for Jt and NSC Matters, 5 Aug 66, subj: World-Wide U.S. Mil Posture; JCSM-506-66 (TS), 5 Aug 66.

8. Memo (TS), J-3 to JCS, 17 Aug 66, subj: Arc Light Planning; memo (TS), Col D.H. King, Asst Chief, War Planning Div, DCS/P&O to Dir of Pers Planning et al, 23 Aug 66, subj: B-52 Ops in SEA.

9. Memo (TS), Wheless to Deps, Dirs, and Chiefs of Comparable Ofcs, 17 Aug 66, subj: Actions Necessary to Determine AF Capability to Meet CINCPAC's CY 66/67 Rqmts; memo (C), Wheless to same addressees, 8 Sep 66, same subj.

10. Memo (TS), Brig Gen E.A. McDonald, Dep Dir of Plans for War Plans to CSAF, 1 Nov 66, subj: Force Deployments to PACOM to Meet CY 1967 Rqmts, w/atch (TS), Background Paper on USAF Capability to Provide TFS for SEA.

11. Memo (TS), Col F. J. Coleman, Asst Dep Dir for War Plans to CSAF, 22 Sep 66, subj: CINCPAC CY 1966 Adjusted Force Rqmts and CY 1967 Force Rqmts; memo (TS), McDonald to CSAF, 1 Nov 66, w/atch (TS), Background Paper on CINCPAC CY 66/67 Add-on Rqmts: Deployment Issue Papers; memo (S), SECDEF to Chmn JCS, 5 Aug 66, subj: CINCPAC CY 1966 Adjusted Rqmts and 1967 Force Rqmts.

12. Hist (TS), Dir/Plans, Jul-Dec 66, pp 353-54; memo (TS), McDonald to CSAF, 1 Nov 66, w/atch (TS), Background Paper on SEA Air Prog; JCSM-613-66 (TS), 24 Sep 66, w/atch (TS), Apps A and B.

13. Memo (TS), McDonald to CSAF, 1 Nov 66, w/atch (TS), Background Paper on CINCPAC CY 66/67 Add-on Rqmts: Deployment Issue Papers; memo (S), SECDEF to Chmn JCS, 6 Oct 66, subj: CINCPAC CY 66 and CY 67 Force Rqmts w/atch (S), 28 Deployment Issue Papers; memo (TS), Rheinbold to CSAF, 8 Oct 66, same subj: memo (TS), Col F. W. Vetter, Mil Asst to SAF, 18 Oct 66, subj: SOD Trip; memo (TS), Lt Col G. S. Thomas, Tac Div, Dir/Ops to CSAF, 28 Nov 66, subj: Employment of Art and Naval Gunfire, SEA; JCSM-736-66 (TS), 29 Nov 66.

14. Memo (TS), Col W. F. Scott, Asst Chief for Unilateral Matters, War Planning Div, DCS/P&O to CSAF, 30 Sep 66, subj: World-Wide Mil Posture; JCSM-646-66 (TS), 7 Oct 66.

15. Hist (S), Dir/Ops, Jul-Dec 66, p 257.

16. Memo (TS), Scott to CSAF, 30 Sep 66; JCSM-646-66 (TS), 7 Oct 66; memo (TS), Clay to CSAF, 17 Sep 66, subj: Capabilities Planning Conf, w/atch (TS), Rprt on CINCPAC's CY 1966/1967 Force Rqmts; Hist (TS), Dir/Plans, Jul-Dec 66, pp 416-17; memo (U), Gen B. K. Holloway, Vice CSAF to DCS/P&O et al, 12 Sep 66, subj: Pilot Manning Study Gp; memo (C), Lt Gen H. M. Wade, DCS/P to DCS/P&R et al, 3 Oct 66, subj: Pilot Rqmts for SEA; Hist (C), Hq TAC, Jan-Jun 66, p 200.

## Chapter V

1. Msg 68984 (S), CINCPACAF to CSAF, 8 Oct 66; Wash Post, 11 Oct 66; Balt Sun, 10 Oct 66.

2. Memo (TS), Wheless to Deps, Dirs, and Chiefs of Comparable Ofcs, 17 Aug 66; ltr (TS), CINCPAC to JCS, 20 Oct 66, subj: CINCPAC CY 66-67 Force Rqmts Capabilities Prog, w/atch (TS), 3 vols; Balt Sun, 10 Oct 66.

3. Memo (TS), Coleman to CSAF, 28 Nov 66, subj: Deployments to SEA and Other PACOM Areas, w/atch (TS), Background Paper on Proposed Force Deployments to PACOM; msg 68984 (TS), CINCPACAF to CSAF, 8 Oct 66; ltr (TS), CINCPAC to JCS, 20 Oct 66, w/atch (TS), 3 vols; memo (S), SECDEF to SAF, 13 Jul 66, subj: Replacement for A-1 Attrition; memo (S), SECDEF to Secys of Mil Depts et al, 1 Aug 66, subj: SEA Deployment Plan #3, change through #9; The Journal of Mil Asst (S), Jun 66, p 175.

4. Msg 68984 (S), CINCPACAF to CSAF, 8 Oct 66; ltr (TS), CINCPAC to JCS, 20 Oct 66.

5. Ltr (TS), CINCPAC to JCS, 22 Oct 66, subj: Eval of Force Availabilities, w/atch (TS), Hq MACV Rprt, 16 Oct 66, no subj: JCS 2343/855-25 (TS), 1 Nov 66; Hist (S), Hq MACV, 1966, pp 638-39.

6. Hist (S), Dir/Plans, Jul-Dec 66, pp 360-61; ltr (TS), CINCPAC to JCS, 23 Oct 66, subj: RVN Force Rqmts/Capabilities and Piaster Force Levels, w/atch (TS), Hq MACV rprt, undated; JCS 2343/855-25 (TS), 1 Nov 66.

7. Memo (TS), McDonald to CSAF, 1 Nov 66, w/atch (TS), Background Paper on USAF Capability to Provide TFS for SEA; memo (TS), McDonald to CSAF, 1 Nov 66, subj: Force Deployments to PACOM to Meet CY 67 Rqmts.

8. JCSM-702-66 (TS), 4 Nov 66.

9. JCS 2343/855-25 (TS), 1 Nov 66; JCSM-702-66 (TS), 4 Nov 66.

10. Memo (TS), SECDEF to Secys of Mil Depts et al, 18 Nov 66, subj: SEA Deployment Prog 4.

11. Memo (TS), SECDEF to JCS, 11 Nov 65; memo (TS), SECDEF to Secys of Mil Depts et al, 18 Nov 66, subj: SEA Deployment Prog 4.

12. Hist (TS), Dir/Plans, Jul-Dec 66, pp 35-37; CM-1839-66 (TS), 17 Oct 66; CSAFM-R-30-66 (TS), 12 Oct 66; memo (TS), SAF to SECDEF, 7 Nov 66, subj: Pacific Trip Action Items; JCS 2343/939 (TS), 26 Oct 66; memo (TS), by W. H. Stokes, Intl Affairs Div, Dir of Plans for Policy, DCS/P&O 19 Oct 66, subj: Arc Light Basing; Sup to Daily Staff Digest (S), 28 Dec 66; memo (TS), SAF to SECDEF, 19 Nov 66, subj: B-52 Basing in SEA, in OSAF; N.Y. Times, 18 Oct-3 Nov 66; JCS 2343/932-1 (S), 30 Nov 66.

13. Memo (TS), Col D. G. Cooper, Ofc Dep Dir of Plans for War Plans, DCS/P&O to CSAF, 28 Nov 66, subj: Deployments to SEA and Other PACOM Areas, w/atch (TS), Background Paper on Proposed Force Deployments to PACOM.

14. JCSM-739-66 (TS), 2 Dec 66; memo (S), SAF to SECDEF, 6 Oct 66, no subj.

15. JCSM-739-66 (TS), 2 Dec 66; Hist (S), Dir/Plans, Jul-Dec 66, p 361; memo (TS), Cooper to CSAF, 28 Nov 66; JCSM-739-66 (TS), 2 Dec 66; CSAF-L-66 (S), 9 Dec 66; memo (S), SAF to SECDEF, 6 Oct 66, no subj.

16. Memo (TS), SECDEF to Chmn JCS, 9 Dec 66, subj: Deployments to SEA and Other PACOM Areas.

17. CM-2015-66 (S), 22 Dec 66; Hist (S), Dir/Plans, pp 338-39; ltr (S), CINCPAC to JCS, 30 Dec 66, subj: CY 67 A/C Mun Allocations, w/atch (S), PACOM CY 67 Air Mun Allocations.

18. USAF Mgt Summary (S), 6 Jan 67, p 21 and 3 Feb 67, p 8.

19. Memo (TS), McDonald to Dir/Plans, 3 Jan 67, subj: Progress Eval, SEA; memo (S), Col G.S. Stubbs, Dep Dir for Policy, Dir/Plans to Dir/Plans, DCS/P&O, 8 Feb 67, subj: Analysis of Ground Ops--1966; Stat Data (U), from OSD Ofc of Public Affairs; memo (S), Lambert to AFCHO, 15 May 66, subj: Draft Hist Study.

## GLOSSARY

| | |
|---|---|
| AB | Air Base |
| A/C | Aircraft |
| ACCC | Airborne Command Control Center |
| AFCHO | USAF Historical Division Liaison Office |
| Aflds | Airfields |
| AGIL | Air-Ground Illumination |
| Apps | Appendices |
| Appns | Appropriations |
| ARDF | Airborne Radio Direction Finding |
| Art | Artillery |
| ASD | Assistant Secretary of Defense |
| Atch | Attached |
| | |
| Bns | Battalions |
| BOD | Beneficial Occupancy Date |
| | |
| CIA | Central Intelligence Agency |
| CINCPAC | Commander-in-Chief, Pacific |
| CINCPACAF | Commander-in-Chief, Pacific Air Forces |
| CM | Chairman's Memo |
| CMCM | |
| COMUSMACV | Commander, U.S. Military Assistance Command, Vietnam |
| Const | Construction |
| CSAF | Chief of Staff, Air Force |
| CSAFM | Chief of Staff Air Force Memo |
| CVA | Attack Carrier Aircraft |
| CY | Calendar Year |
| | |
| DAF | Department of the Air Force |
| DCS/P | Deputy Chief of Staff, Personnel |
| DCS/P&O | Deputy Chief of Staff, Plans and Operations |
| DCS/P&R | Deputy Chief of Staff, Programs and Resources |
| Dep | Deputy |
| DIA | Defense Intelligence Agency |
| Dir/Aerospace Progs | Director of Aerospace Programs |
| Dir/Pers Planning | Directorate of Personnel Planning |
| Dir/Plans | Directorate of Plans |
| Dir/Ops | Directorate of Operations |
| Dir/Trnsp | Directorate of Transportation |
| DMZ | Demilitarized Zone |
| DOD | Department of Defense |
| | |
| ECM | Electronic Countermeasures |
| ELINT | Electronic Intelligence |
| Eng | Engineer |

| | |
|---|---|
| Estb | Established |
| Eval | Evaluation |
| FAC | Forward Air Controller |
| FWMAF | Free World Military Assistance Forces |
| Gp | Group |
| Hist | History |
| I&L | Installations and Logistics |
| ISA | International Security Affairs |
| JCSM | Joint Chief of Staff Memo |
| Jt | Joint |
| Log | Logistics |
| MACV | Military Assistance Command, Vietnam |
| Man | Maneuver |
| Mil | Military |
| Mun | Munitions |
| NATO | North Atlantic Treaty Organization |
| NSC | National Security Council |
| NVN | North Vietnam |
| Ops | Operations |
| OSAF | Office, Secretary of the Air Force |
| OSD | Office, Secretary of Defense |
| PACAF | Pacific Air Forces |
| PACOM | Pacific Command |
| PAVN | People's Army, Vietnam |
| Pers | Personnel |
| POL | Petroleum, Oil, and Lubricants |
| Pres | President |
| Proc | Procurement |
| Prog | Program |

| | |
|---|---|
| RP | Route Package |
| Rprt | Report |
| R/T | Rolling Thunder |
| RTU | Replacement Training Unit |
| Rqmts | Requirements |
| | |
| SA | Systems Analysis |
| SAF | Secretary of the Air Force |
| SAFIO | Secretary of the Air Force Information Office |
| SEA | Southeast Asia |
| SECDEF | Secretary of Defense |
| SM | Secretary's Memo |
| SOD | Secretary of Defense |
| Stat | Statistic |
| Sup | Supply, Supplement |
| SVN | South Vietnam |
| | |
| TAC | Tactical Air Command |
| Tac | Tactical |
| TFS | Tactical Fighter Squadron |
| | |
| UE | Unit Equipment |
| USAFE | United States Air Force, Europe |
| | |
| VC | Viet Cong |
| VN | Vietnam |
| VNAF | Vietnamese Air Force |

## DISTRIBUTION

### HQ USAF

1. SAF-OS
2. SAF-US
3. SAF-FM
4. SAF-RD
5. SAF-IL
6. SAF-GC
7. SAF-LL
8. SAF-OI
9. SAF-OIX
10. SAF-AAR
11. AFCCSSA
12. AFCSA
13. AFCSAI
14. AFCVC
15. AFCVS
16. AFBSA
17. AFESS
18. AFGOA
19. AFIIS
20. AFJAG
21. AFNIN
22. AFAAF
23. AFABF
24. AFADA
25. AFADS
26. AFAMA
27. AFODC
28. AFOAP
29. AFOAPB
30. AFOAPD
31. AFOAPDB
32. AFOAPEB
33. AFOCC
34. AFOCE
35. AFOCEH
36. AFOMO
37. AFOMOA
38. AFPDC
39. AFPMC
40. AFRDC
41. AFRDD
42. AFRDQ
43. AFRDQR
44. AFRRP
45. AFRST
46. AFSDC
47. AFSLP
48. AFSLPB
49. AFSME
50. AFSMS
51. AFSPD
52. AFSPP
53. AFSSS
54. AFSTP
55. AFXDC
56. AFXDO
57. AFXOP
58. AFXOP-A
59. AFXOPF
60. AFXOPFH
61. AFXOPFI
62. AFXOPFL
63. AFXOPX
64. AFXPD
65. AFXPDA
66. AFXPDC
67. AFXPDF
68. AFXPDG
69. AFXPDI
70. AFXPDO
71. AFXPDP
72. AFXPDR

### MAJOR COMMANDS

73. AAC
74. ADC
76-75. AFCS
76-78. AFLC
79-80. AFSC
81. ATC
82. CAC
83-84. MAC
85. OAR
86-88. PACAF
89-90. SAC
91-92. TAC
93. USAFA
94. USAFE
95. USAFSO
96. USAFSS

### OTHER

97-98. RAND
99-101. ASI (ASHAF-A)
102. CHECO (DOAC)-7 AF
103-115. AFCHO (Stock).

Printed in Great Britain
by Amazon